CHINESE BRUSHSTROKES

CHINESE BRUSHSTROKES
Stories of China

by Sandra Hutchison

TURNSTONE PRESS

Turnstone Press
607-100 Arthur Street
Winnipeg, Manitoba
Canada R3B 1H3

Turnstone Press gratefully acknowledges the assistance of the
Canada Council and the Manitoba Arts Council.

Cover artwork: Joseph Lo

Design: Manuela Dias

This book was printed and bound in Canada
by Friesens for Turnstone Press.

Canadian Cataloguing in Publication Data

Hutchison, Sandra Lynn, 1954–

Chinese brushstrokes

ISBN 0-88801-209-8

1. Hutchison, Sandra Lynn, 1954–   2. Canadians -
China - Biorgraphy.   3. English teachers - China -
Biography.   4. Teachers, foreign - China - Biography.
5. China - Social life and customs - 1976–
6. China - History - 1976 - I. Title.

PR55.H88A3 1996   951.05'8'092   C96-920113-3

For my parents

Contents

Notes

The surname comes first in Chinese names, and I have kept to this system here.

Throughout the book, pinyin, the official system of romanization in the People's Republic of China, has been used, except when another spelling was thought to be more familiar to the English reader.

The people who figure in the stories are real but their names have been changed.

Acknowledgements

I would like to thank all my students and teachers in China for so generously sharing their knowledge and so steadfastly offering their friendship over the past decade.

Professor Li Yongfang of Anhui University answered numerous questions about Chinese language and culture, and refreshed my memory about places and place names. Ms. Ji Shuren read the manuscript for factual errors, corrected pinyin spellings, and gave much encouragement in the final stages of the manuscript.

The Ontario Arts Council provided a generous and timely works-in-progress grant to support the completion of the manuscript. Manuela Dias, the production manager, was faithfully present at every stage and in every detail of the production of the book. I would also like to thank my copy-editor Marilyn Morton for her meticulous work on the manuscript.

Many friends and colleagues answered questions and offered help with various details of the manuscript, and I would like to thank them for checking facts and providing information.

I would like especially to thank my own family. Each one offered unfailing support and encouragement in his or her own way. I am deeply indebted to my parents for their assistance, in ways both large and small, during the months I spent in Toronto writing the first draft. Without their help, the manuscript would never have been completed. A special thanks is also owing to my husband, Richard Hollinger, who spent many hours reading and editing the manuscript as we moved between countries. His loving attention to every detail of the book contributed immeasurably to its completion.

May the East and West clasp hands together.

—'Abdu'l-Bahá

Prologue

"BUT THOSE WHO VALUE wisdom or beauty, or even the simple enjoyment of life, will find more of these things in China than in the distracted and turbulent West. . . ." I looked out the window. Below me brooded a vast darkness. I could not guess the hour; North American time had lost all relevance. I wondered if we were flying over the Yellow Sea yet. I continued reading: "I wish I could hope that China, in return for our scientific knowledge, may give us something of her large tolerance and contemplative peace of mind." Neither mystic nor guru had penned these words; they had been written by the English philosopher Bertrand Russell, who had travelled to China in 1920 to lecture at the National University of Peking. But neither statement resonated with the objectivity of the philosopher; instead, they struck that chord of yearning and awe sometimes sounded in the notes of travellers. I tried to imagine what had inspired such musings.

Could it have been a classical Chinese garden Russell had unexpectedly come across in his wanderings around the campus of the university? Could it have been a professor of philosophy he had met who began each day at dawn with brush in hand and rice paper and a pot of black ink before him, penning Chinese characters in his favourite style of calligraphy? I imagined Russell on an early morning walk, stumbling upon a group of literature professors dancing their way through the meditative ballet of tai chi. But Russell had visited China in the 1920s. That was decades ago. The China he had known could well have vanished completely. I strained my eyes once again to catch a glimmer of light, the hint of a shape. Nothing. Still a sea of pitch-black. No clues. No premonitions. And there was no one to query. All around me, my fellow-travellers, mostly Chinese, were wrapped in a deep sleep.

As they slept, I meditated. Not far into my meditation, a movie screen rolled down in front of me, and onto it were projected some of the strangest images I had ever seen. The film was called *Journey to the West*. It wasn't about the mass exodus of Chinese scholars, young and old, to America in recent years to learn Western science and the latest technologies, but about another journey to the "West" made long ago by a creature both mischievous and holy, a creature remarkably like a human being. The film was based on the adventures of the Monkey King on his travels to India.

The Monkey King, I found out later, is a mythic figure who was popularized by a novel written sometime during the Ming dynasty. The first seven chapters of this hundred-chapter book describe the birth of the Monkey King and how he acquires magical powers, creates a riot in heaven, and destroys the heavenly palace of the Emperor. Eventually, the Monkey King is subdued by the Buddha and given the assignment of escorting and protecting the monk Tripitaka on his journey to the "West"—in fact India—in search of the Buddhist scriptures, which he plans to bring back to China.

It was an interesting story. Was that what it was like for the Chinese going abroad now, I wondered. Did the West seem to them a place replete with sacred knowledge hermetically sealed in the scroll of North American life? Did the search for ways to acquire Western technology, in its most sophisticated forms, such as satellites and spaceships, or even in its most banal manifestations, such as the Sony Walkman, have for them the quality of a quest? Or was it something else the Chinese were looking for in our society, some more abstract principles or more concrete material benefits?

The film had been over for an hour, but I could not sleep. Now we were flying over the Yellow Sea, the air hostess announced in Chinese and then in barely comprehensible English. I remembered the approach to Shanghai from my whirlwind tour of China the previous autumn. Before long, the green strips of field, the rice paddies, and the complex water system sustaining them would come into view. Then Shanghai would emerge, a grey blot of urban life randomly splashed on the vast canvas of green that is China, a nation which from the air looks like a huge and infinitely variegated garden.

I looked out the window at the Yellow Sea below. The moon was shedding a glimmer of light on the surging waves. Suddenly, a young Chinese man interrupted my reverie with these words: "Ninety-five percent crash."

"What?" I asked.

"The chance, mmm . . . , ninety-five percent . . . mmm . . . crash . . . ," he repeated.

The same screen onto which the curious tale of holiness and human frailty had been projected rolled down in front of me, and the safety procedures, in crisp Mandarin, played over and over again at high speed.

The air hostess came around to give me and another foreign teacher instructions in faltering English. "Preese fahsten yowr bets. Lemove ahl jewry. Prace ahl yowr berongings under the seet. Lemove yowr shoes. Assume clash position."

A middle-aged cadre to my right bent forward over the

3

new ghetto-blaster he held in his arms. His shoes were still on his feet, though he had no jewelry to remove. He lit a cigarette and smoked quietly as the plane descended. Turning in my direction, he laughed and nodded vigorously. The next thing I knew we had landed safely on the tarmac in Beijing.

The crash-landing had been a myth generated by the oral tradition of communicating news. Although two of the plane's tires had blown, the chances of a crash had been only five percent, not ninety-five percent. But passed from mouth to mouth, the words had created a new truth that had quickly evolved from fact to legend. It didn't matter whether it were true or not: people felt it to be true and experienced it as truth. But far from fretting or writing last wills and testaments as I had once read a Japanese man on a doomed jet had done, the Chinese passengers had laughed. It was exciting, and, besides, there was absolutely nothing you could do about it. Many had gone before us and many would come after us. We were part of history.

To be part of history—perhaps this was the dream that had spurred so many Western travellers Chinaward? Silk and religion—was it really these that drove a Marco Polo or a Matteo Ricci eastward? Or was it the desire to become a link in the longest human line we know, the oldest living civilization on earth? History: the Chinese carried it within them. After my year in China, I would too. One balmy night in April I would be awakened by the sound of students banging pots and shouting slogans in our school basketball court. Two months later, I would leave China at the urging of the Canadian Embassy in Beijing, with images of bent and broken bicycles and blood-spattered shirts engraved forever in my mind.

But on my first night in China, I did not think of such things. I saw only the light shed by the sliver of a new moon shining down upon us, myself and a fellow passenger from Canada, an artist named Penny. From the Beijing airport, we had been bussed to a modest hotel in the suburbs to sleep until the next morning when we would be ferried by airbus back to Shanghai, our original destination. But Penny and I were too excited to sleep. Penny was of Chinese descent, and it was her first time in China. She had come to study printmaking and Chinese brushstroke painting at the Zhejiang Academy of Fine Arts in Hangzhou. Penny planned to immerse herself in the ancient culture and arts of her ancestors.

When Penny asked me why I had come to China, I thought for a minute. I told her I would be teaching English literature at a university in Hefei, the capital city of Anhui Province: graduate courses in Shakespeare, Canadian Literature, and Modern Poetry, and undergraduate courses in British Literature. I told her I had come as a teacher. But that was not entirely true. The truth was as Bertrand Russell had written many decades before: "When I went to China, I went to teach; but every day that I stayed I thought less of what I had to teach them and more of what I had to learn from them."

"Contemplative peace of mind"—a year after my return from China, I was still meditating on Russell's words. The China I had known was grey, soot filled, bleak, and depressing. It bore little resemblance to Bertrand Russell's China. Yet why, when I thought of my time in China, did I remember only the music of the rain falling on the leaves of the *ba-jiao* trees outside my window, and the Chinese garden adorning the courtyard of the Foreign Guest-house, with its quaint, arched bridges overshadowing glistening ponds of serene, white water lilies? I remembered the Lake of Tears, an algae-infested, man-made lake the university officials had somehow decided was essential to the beautification of the campus, shimmering as the students walked hand in hand around it on moonlit nights, and the old people swaying to some ancient, inner music as they practised tai chi on its shores at dawn.

One night, about a year after I returned from China, I had a dream. My Chinese teacher was taking me on a train back, far back, into time. As we travelled, I passed by all the people who had been part of my past—grade-school friends, comrades from my young adulthood, fellow travellers from more recent times—until I arrived at a beautiful garden in the classical Chinese style. The train stopped and I disembarked. I passed through an arched doorway into the garden. A brushstroke master waited to greet me. A room had been prepared for me. With a wave of his hand, he gestured his welcome. I entered the room and sat down. Then I took up my brush and I began to paint.

THE VALLEY OF SEARCH

"When you pray to God in China, nobody answers." Wu Li was not expressing an attitude shaped by a lifetime's immersion in Marxist philosophy; she was speaking from experience. Many of my other colleagues and my students shared her feeling. It would never have occurred to them to call upon God, that anthropomorphic figure who looks after all our needs. It was a Western notion, culturally distant, incomprehensible.

In Taoism, the concept of a deity is closer to a force, a pervasive spirit or energy manifesting itself in the harmonious workings of the physical creation. But few Chinese I met seemed interested, let alone versed, in China's ancient philosophies. Nor did it occur to them to turn to the "god" upon which the People's Republic of China had been founded: communism. The Cultural Revolution had called such worship into question, and the Tiananmen tragedy had marked the final shattering of the idols. I will never forget the words of my fellow teacher Hu Xiaomei after the crushing of the students in Tiananmen Square: "Perhaps what China needs is a new philosophy, a universal religion."

The cynicism of my fellow teachers about Mao Zedong

Thought was widespread. During the much-hated but compulsory weekly Political Study class, one teacher I knew used to read classical Chinese poetry. More than once, Hu Xiaomei skipped class altogether to laugh with me as, prompted by a yoga program broadcast live from Thailand, we contorted our bodies in the most unnatural of positions. One scene I came across in my ramblings about the city struck me as an especially apt emblem of the mood of my colleagues. While searching for a book in a neighbouring university library, I discovered a life-sized portrait of Mao propped unceremoniously under an abandoned stair-well just gathering dust.

Yet for my colleagues, politics still impinged on the most personal aspects of life. Politics decreed, for example, that Chinese Catholics should worship independently of the Vatican. Politics also decreed that it was acceptable for the Chinese to honour, once again, their ancient traditions. With a fellow foreign teacher, I travelled overnight by train on a "hard-seat" to Qufu, the home of Confucius, to watch the ancient ceremonies celebrating the Master's birthday. More than a thousand people had travelled from all over China to attend the celebration, and they looked on with fascination as a handful of officiants performed the ancient rituals.

There were still Christian missionaries in China, I soon learned, placed by missionary organizations billed as English-language teaching services. Occasionally, the missionaries would leave their posts for weekends of spiritual renewal in Shanghai or other major cities. As the dean of the Foreign Languages Department explained to me, the Chinese government and the university administration thought the missionaries quite harmless. Christianity, I was told by other colleagues, was simply not suited to Chinese conditions or attractive to the Chinese sensibility. In their minds, there was no danger of a mass influx into such a religion. Still, the missionaries received a rousing welcome whenever they attended services at the local church, where aging believers, trained in evangelical Protestantism, still remembered all the words to soul-stirring hymns popular in the early twentieth century.

In those places where no missionary had ever been I was

privileged to witness some of the traditional practices still resonant with meaning for so many Chinese. About the time of the Qing Ming Festival, during which families honour their ancestors by tending their graves, one of my students and I cycled to the countryside. The apple trees bloomed, white and fragrant, and the wildflowers blew all across the local mountain, Dashu Shan. As Cao Meihua and I approached the mountain, we saw it was crawling with students out to enjoy the bracing spring air and pick the wildflowers. We were not in the mood for crowds, so we hid our bicycles in an orchard and walked in the opposite direction, towards a distant village. We walked and walked. Eventually, we got close enough to the village to read the characters painted on the red banners freshly pasted on either side of the doors of each home to welcome in the new year.

On the far edge of the village, we passed a family walking down a footpath in the direction of the open fields. Curious to see where the parents and their one son were going, we followed at a distance. Before long, the family stopped in front of a cluster of burial mounds, all topped with bright red ribbons. We watched as the family members performed the rituals of ancestor worship. The ceremony was simple, but I was moved to see the young son bow down in front of the graves of his grandparents and lay red paper money there. After kowtowing several times, the young boy lit a small packet of firecrackers. The faces of the family remained solemn throughout the ceremony. After the family had left, Cao Meihua and I silently approached the graves. The smoke from the exploded firecrackers lingered in the air, gradually drifting off over the rice paddies, leaving me with an inexplicable feeling of loss.

I doubt many would describe the Chinese as a mystical people. They seemed to look on mystical experiences with condescension and on mystics with pity, as you might look on someone who has been betrayed in love. Still, the rituals of faith intrigued many of my students and colleagues. Hu Xiaomei was entranced by a Buddhist funeral ceremony we saw when we visited a local temple. Cao Meihua, assuming that every foreigner in China was a missionary, wanted to know whether I prayed in my room every day. And when I returned from travels in India, after the Spring

9

Sandra Hutchison

Festival vacation, my students listened wide-eyed to my description of ritual bathing in the Ganges River on the occasion of the Kumbh Mela, or holy dip. For many of my friends, religion held an exotic allure. To me, it seemed they were travelling on the steed of curiosity through the Valley of Search. Did they seek the beloved Layli in the dust, as the Majnun of Love is said to have done? Maybe not. But they did seek, and in their own way, they found.

Joy to the World

IN HEFEI, THE NIGHT before Christmas is the quietest of all nights. A light snow might fall and a friend come to walk with you under the wintry stars. It will be just the two of you strolling by the Lake of Tears. There, the ice will shimmer in the moonlight, reminding you of a backyard skating rink your father once made somewhere in the Canadian North by pouring sheet after icy sheet of water on the lawn until in the morning there appeared, magically, the greatest skating rink on earth, where you could become a figure skater, your father's favourite daughter. On the night before Christmas, the Lake of Tears looks a little like that.

When Hu Xiaomei came to my door two nights before Christmas, I thought she had come to propose such a walk. I imagined she had come to invite me to her home for *babaofan* (Eight Treasures Pudding), and after enjoying this special holiday pudding we would circle the lake, our talk filled with peaceful thoughts of my home in Canada and of her home in Shanghai. I expected it would be a time of special communion between two close friends, each equally alone—Hu because of her disdain as a sophisticated Shanghainese for the provincial university where we taught, and me because I was far from home. But when she spoke, I could see that Christmas held no significance whatsoever for Hu Xiaomei.

I doubt that Hu Xiaomei would have even dropped by that night if it had not been for her dilemma. There were only two churches in Hefei: the Catholic Church and the "other church," as it was usually called, a non-denominational church, probably at one time Protestant. Hu Xiaomei's dilemma had to do with the "other church," where an elaborate Christmas program, including a nativity play, the surprise arrival of Santa Claus, arias by Bach and Handel, and Christmas carols in Mandarin, was being planned. But so far there were no Christmas carols in English. It wasn't really Hu Xiaomei's problem. Christmas meant nothing to her, except as the night of the annual third-year students' class party. But a Christian friend who had helped her get a job moonlighting at one of the city's night schools had cornered Hu, begging for the name of any foreigner who could sing. As we strolled through the lightly falling snow she asked me, "Do you have any idea who might help?"

I had only one night to practise. It was late, but Hu Xiaomei offered to help me. Inside my rooms, Hu cuddled up by my lone space-heater. I made us each a cup of Chinese tea. We drank in silence, savouring the stillness of the night.

"It is very romantic outside," Hu said at last. "It makes me think of 'Stopping by Woods on a Snowy Evening.' " She quoted, "Whose woods these are I think I know. / His house is in the village, though. . . ."

Every one of the teachers and students of English in the Foreign Languages Department knew the poem by heart. I looked out the window at the *ba-jiao* grove, dried, brown, and brittle, and then at the Chinese garden, long ago laid to rest by the whistling winds of autumn. Snow fell intermittently, the huge flakes swallowed up instantly by the grey, porous pavement, leaving no trace of winter behind. The soot from burning coal blackened the air. The scene was the furthest thing I could imagine from the New England woods where Robert Frost had stopped with his horse.

Hu paused and sipped her tea. We returned to the subject: which carol should I sing? "Joy to the World" was the only song suited for the occasion, Hu argued, and even though it was an English carol, she could see no reason why I couldn't slip in a verse or two in Chinese for effect. We stayed up into the early morning hours practising. I pronounced the words and Hu corrected my Mandarin, with her singsong, heavily articulated vowels and consonants weaving in and out of my dreamy half-sleep. In a couple of hours, I had mastered every sound in the verses we had translated. Hu trudged home to Teachers' Dormitory Number Four for a few hours of sleep before classes the next morning.

The day before Christmas dawned grey, bleak, and miserable, the wettest day of the year so far. Hu Xiaomei passed me a blue plastic poncho when she dropped by my classroom. It was supposed to rain that evening, she explained. For the students, the day was like any other. No special electricity charged the air, even when after classes Zhao Youbin, one of the few boys in the school who had been to the United States, fell down on the floor at the back of our classroom to demonstrate the break-dance routine he planned to do that evening at the class Christmas party. Too preoccupied with the rain to think much about the party, in the unheated classroom the students shuffled to keep warm. At five o'clock, they marched stiff-legged, a phalanx of bright umbrellas, to the cafeteria, where they sat chatting, eating their rice, and pulling their jackets tightly around them against the cold.

Several classes held Christmas parties that night in the

mostly dark Foreign Languages Building. From a distance, the lit classrooms glowed, like small candles bobbing in a vast sea of darkness. Inside the third-year students' classroom, sunflower seeds dotted the desktops. Students cracked them open and spit the shells on the floor as they laughed and sang songs like "Red River Valley." The top of my desk was strewn with hard fruit candies, and the podium, where I usually stood to deliver my lectures, was gaily decorated with pink, blue, and yellow streamers spilling over its sides and covering the red star of the New China emblazoned on its front. Except for a lengthy classical Chinese love poem recited by Mr. Bao and his girlfriend, Miss Yan, the party wasn't memorable. As I stepped with Hu Xiaomei out of the classroom into the cold drizzle, I could still see the mouth of Party Secretary Shen, his lips rounded in the "O" of "O Holy Night," the carol Hu had taught her class especially for the occasion.

Christmas night, holy night, the most treasured night of my Canadian childhood, and yet in its own way as secular an occasion as it was here in China, since my parents had never been practising Christians. Still, the fragrance of holiness had permeated the air of our two-storey white brick house in Toronto as my father took his annual dose of Dickens's *A Christmas Carol* on television and my mother stuffed and roasted a turkey to be tucked into the trunk of our Ford station wagon the next day and served to the whole family at my grandmother's table. As Hu Xiaomei and I walked towards our bicycles, my mind filled with images from the past: of the family farm, of my brothers, sisters, parents, grandparents, aunts, uncles, and cousins singing carols around my grandmother's home-grown Christmas tree, a pungent Scotch pine. In our extended family, we had all been drawn from far away in those days, as if by some magnetic force, to my grandmother's white, framed farmhouse, moving in a circle of relationships much like the shape made by the mouth of the Party secretary as he sang "O Holy Night."

Hu Xiaomei and I cycled down the dark streets, hooded like the monks of old, our flowing robes of plastic hanging down on either side of our bicycles to protect us from the rain. Hu was saying something about the Christmas carol I was to sing. But in the world of my reverie, her words, subsumed by the darkness of the night and the seemingly endless journey to the church, faded into nothingness, like the raindrops falling beneath the onrushing wheels of our bicycles. We seemed to pass through a timeless world in which we could not get our bearings, through the great, black emptiness of a world without Christmas lights or even street lamps, a world in which the night was neither holy nor silent but filled with a great emptiness that I could not name or define.

As we turned left at the post office, the church came into view. Through its open gate, worshippers spilled out onto the street. Balancing umbrellas or jackets over their heads, they pushed inward towards the warmth and light of the church. Hu Xiaomei led me, bicycle in tow, through the thronging masses, announcing that a foreigner had come from Canada to sing a Christmas carol. I followed Hu Xiaomei, reticent and embarrassed. Wide-eyed and tentative at first, when greeted in Chinese the people opened up like sunflowers basking in the summer light. They smiled, their faces luminous, when I passed, an honoured guest from *waibian* (outside) with a mission to perform on a dark, rainy night. Maybe they thought I was a missionary, the descendant of one of those cultured English ladies who had graced these rooms more than half a century before. Probably to them, any foreigner who lived in Hefei and came to church on a night like this would have to be a missionary.

I passed through a back room filled with rows of desks. At each, a man or a woman, most of them greying and over sixty, sat with an open Bible. In the next room, the organ played and the choir led the congregation in the hymn "He Is My Rock and My Salvation." After the hymn ended, the people settled into the pews, chatting and smiling, not overawed at all by the solemn atmosphere of this holy night. One of the greatest public occasions of the year in the world of these churchgoers, the Christmas celebration was a spectacle to be greedily enjoyed.

The preacher, Pastor Fu, ascended to the pulpit and gave the blessing. The lights went out, and the angel Gabriel came onto the stage carrying a single candle to light his way as he announced to the awestruck Mary the birth of a son called Immanuel. Hu Xiaomei sat, face impassive. The three kings paraded before us. We followed the Magi through the desert, our eyes fixed on a distant star. Together with the lowly shepherds, we watched the flocks of sheep by night. At last, we arrived in Bethlehem itself, to witness the birth of the Christ child. Sitting with me in the front row, Hu Xiaomei remained unmoved. Even the aria from Bach, her favourite Western composer, did not seem to touch her. She looked detached—merely an interested observer.

When the time came for my Christmas carol, Hu Xiaomei grew alert. As I left the pew for the sanctuary, she leaned forward in anticipation. Pastor Fu introduced me: I was a *waiguo pengyou* (foreign friend) and a teacher from one of the local universities, and I had come to sing a foreigner's Christmas carol. According to Hu's plan I would sing the first two verses in English. On the last verse, I would shift to Chinese.

Almost a thousand Chinese peasants and workers, interspersed with a few intellectuals and theology students, sat transfixed. I looked at Hu Xiaomei as I began to sing the English verses. She listened, intent on each word, as if, once uttered, it was a thing to be seen and examined. As I stood in the sanctuary of the church singing, Hu Xiaomei sat in the pew mouthing the words: "Joy to the world, the Lord is come. / Let earth receive her King." I began the Chinese verse. A murmur swept through the crowd. When I had finished singing, one thousand pairs of hands exploded into riotous applause. In the spirit of this holy night, Santa Claus jumped up into the sanctuary just as the applause faded and threw handfuls of candies into the throngs of people, who called out and reached with outstretched arms, each hoping to be a recipient of these small Christmas presents.

By the time I got back to the pew, Hu Xiaomei had withdrawn into her usual posture: the detached onlooker. She rose from her seat and motioned me to follow. No one noticed as we slipped away, Hu Xiaomei holding my hand and guiding me through a crowd of peasants as boisterous and jocund as any in Brueghel's paintings. All around us the cry of "Merry Christmas!" rang, and from the street the church seemed to vibrate with the sound. We climbed onto our bicycles and pedalled out into the dark, rainy night, leaving the lights and exultation of the church behind.

Our bicycle wheels whirred softly, a soothing contrast to the frantic scene in the church. Neither of us was eager to talk. I wondered silently, how had it all seemed to Hu Xiaomei? The swish of the city traffic lay behind us. There were no lights to guide us now, only the keenness of our eyesight in the dark. We turned down the road to the university. Fields stretched on either side of us and the unpaved road grew muddy. Just for a moment, the moon broke through the grey clouds; then it disappeared again.

We were minutes from the campus when I heard the most haunting sound. It came from the lips of Hu Xiaomei: "O Holy Night, / The stars are softly shin–ing." There were no stars, not a single one in the sky, and the rain beat down in a light but steady stream, shrouding the road ahead in a grey, uncertain mist. Still, it was Christmas, and Hu Xiaomei was singing out into the silence of the night. The rain continued falling as we rode on through the vast darkness.

Seventh Son of a Seventh Son

"DR. HA QISEN?" The nervous young man asked me as he held out his sweaty palm. I grasped his hand. "Ha is a Hui name," he continued. "My mother is a Hui. From the village of Taihe. Her name is also Ha."

"Please come in," I replied. "Yes, Ha Qisen is my name. How can I help you? Would you like some tea?"

One of the other foreign teachers at our university had mentioned that someone from a teachers' college up north would be coming to see me. Dan had been invited there to lecture on the Bible the first week of November, but had come down with a cold and suggested me as a substitute. Now a tall, curly haired young man stood at my door, and his name was Ding Liang.

Several days after my first meeting with Ding Liang, a black car pulled up to the door of the Foreign Guesthouse, and Ding Liang and I set off on a journey through some of the least-visited counties of the province. A number of the areas we would be driving through were still off limits to foreign visitors, Ding explained apologetically. He wondered if I would mind not looking out the window. I quickly averted my eyes from the passing countryside and fixed them on the only point of distraction I could find: his face.

"What would you like to do instead?" I asked, wondering how we were going to pass the six-hour car drive without looking out the window.

"Would you like me to sing for you?" he asked shyly. I politely nodded my head and braced myself for a long car ride. Ding Liang closed his big, round eyes and began to sing.

What emanated from the mouth of Ding Liang was manna for the hungry opera-lover. Aria followed aria, the melodies and the stories behind them so moving that the tears rolled down Ding Liang's cheeks, and I, oblivious to the swiftly passing forbidden countryside, asked him to tell me the story of how he had learned to sing.

A child star with a travelling Huangmei Opera troupe in the north of the province, the young Ding Liang had spent his childhood on the road, dressed as a very young soldier in the Great Proletarian Cultural Revolution. Because of his youth and size, he had often played female roles. The youngest member of the troupe, he was always the star of the performance, but after it was over he had found himself alone, a lonely child, comforted by the arms of strange women, beautiful women dressed in costumes and singing songs more curious than even the imagination of a child could conjure. Ding was the child of *The White-Haired Girl* and *Red Detachment of Women*.

"Tell me more about yourself," I urged him when he had finished the story of his boyhood.

"How can I say," he answered, "when I myself don't know who I am?" I had been in China long enough to know that such a statement always preceded a much-relished personal confession, and so I waited silently. "I am," he continued, filling in the silence as a skilled hostess discreetly fills an empty cup of tea, "a seventh son of a seventh son. I am . . . I am . . ."—he paused to give full weight to his confession—"a Muslin."

"A Muslin?" I asked. "Don't you mean 'Muslim'?"

"Yes," he replied, not hearing the distinction. "I am a Muslin. Everyone knows it. You can ask anyone at the college. They will all tell you the same. They think I am strange because of it. You'll see. You'll see."

"And what do you think about being a Muslin?" I asked, deciding to adopt Ding's pronunciation.

"My father reads Arabic. He wears a skullcap under his Mao cap. Lately, he has been going to the mosque again to pray."

"What does your father pray for?" I asked.

"How should I know about such things?" Ding said. "I am only the seventh son of a seventh son of a Muslin. I want to live according to my own ideas." He paused and then continued, "So don't ask me what my father prays for. I do not know. Maybe you can answer that question better than me. You are a Christian, aren't you?"

"No," I said, "I am a Ha, and, as you know, Has are not Christians. Maybe I am a Muslin too."

It didn't matter to Ding whether it was true or not. It was the gesture that counted. "Then we will always be together?" he asked. I nodded.

The next day I was scheduled to give a lecture on the Bible as literature. I arrived at the classroom with my notes in my hand. About halfway through my survey of some of the different genres of literature in the Old and New Testaments—the poetry, the wisdom literature, the prophetic books—I realized I had made the worst possible mistake. How could these students, minds honed by Marxist philosophy, possibly take the Book of Revelation seriously? Vague and esoteric, its symbolism obscure and fantastic, the vision of John had no practical application. I decided to rush through the material I had prepared and open the class to questions. Too shy to speak in class, the students sent scraps of folded paper to the front of the room until I had enough to cover the podium. They wanted to know:

> What do you think of Adam eating the fruit of the Tree of Knowledge? Don't you think that the disobeyance is sometimes a good thing? What's the main theme to research in the Bible? Could you talk about it briefly? Could you tell us why the Bible is influencing all over the world? Do you really believe in God? Tell us the reason. Would you please tell us how Christianity prays to the God? Do monks and nuns in Western countries know *qigong* after living in the church for a long time? Could you tell us what revelation Christianity gives to you? What is the relation between the Bible and realities?

Outside the classroom, Ding Liang waited for me. As soon as the last student had left, he flung open the door and struck an operatic pose. "Tomorrow," he announced, "we go to Bordeaux!"

"Bordeaux?" I asked. "You mean, like the city in France?"

"No," he answered, "B-O-Z-H-O-U." He spelled it out carefully for me. "I have a friend who works for the Tourist Bureau there. He is waiting for us. The dean has approved the visit."

"Why Bozhou?"

"Bozhou is famous in Anhui Province."

"For what?"

"For the great doctor of Chinese medicine Hua Tuo, the battleground of General Cao Cao, and the largest opera pavilion outside of Beijing. You will see. And by the way, did you know the population there is ten percent Muslin?"

Ding Liang and I climbed into the university car and headed for a local restaurant. When we arrived, he asked me what I would like to eat.

"Me? I love baozi!" I said, thinking I was pronouncing the name of my favourite kind of steamed bun.

"Baozi? Leopard?" Ding asked, puzzled.

When the waiter came, Ding gave a long order in Chinese. "What did you get us?" I asked.

"Mutton and pilaf and other dishes. It's okay," he added, smiling. "I told him you were a Muslin. . . ."

Had it not been so far from the nearest major city, Bozhou might have been a novel stop for the traveller searching for the mysteries of the Orient. But the route passed through some of the most barren and uninviting territory in China, so the dust of the journey clouded the pleasure of arrival at the destination.

Mr. Yang, Ding's friend and the head of the Tourist Bureau, did his best to revive our interest in Bozhou by taking us on a tour of the modern part of the city. Afterwards, we stopped at Bozhou's newest hotel for lunch. Constructed, it seemed, in the utmost haste, the hotel already looked dilapidated. As we debated where to sit, a busload of German tourists descended on the hotel, jostling with one another for a table in the restaurant and talking loudly about savouring the local dishes. The waiters began to scurry to and fro, seating the Germans according to their preferences, though to me all the tables, with their dingy white imitation-lace tablecloths, looked equally unappealing.

Mr. Yang headed for the door and motioned us to follow. "Come with me," he said. "I will take you to my home."

Mr. Yang led. Ding Liang and I followed. Our route passed through the old city, its streets sinuous, narrow, and made of cobblestones. As we walked, Mr. Yang pointed out sights we would never have seen on an official tour of the city: the pockmarked frontispiece of an old building, now the Bank of China, scarred during the Cultural Revolution by the bullets of rivalling factions; doors on which were tacked, in the custom of Muslims in the area, a small piece of rabbit fur and a strip of red paper inscribed with the name of the family; and neighbourhood cafés crowded with middle-aged and elderly men in white skullcaps drinking tea and smoking cigarettes.

By the time we approached the white, two-storey house in the Middle Eastern style, Ding Liang and I had lost our bearings. Its generous courtyard and large second-floor balcony seemed designed to capture the light and heat of what, given the northern climate, could only be an imaginary sun. "Welcome to my home," said Mr. Yang, bowing almost imperceptibly and ushering us in the door.

An old man in a white skullcap sat just inside the door reading a large book filled with Arabic characters. From the elaborateness of the calligraphy and the careful way he held the book, I concluded that it must be the Qur'an. I glanced at Ding Liang. He looked back at me and nodded slightly in answer to my unspoken question. "Yes," his eyes seemed to say, "the elder Yang is a Muslim."

The elder Yang took us on a tour of the spacious house, while Mrs. Yang finished cooking and serving dishes perfumed with the spices of distant lands. Over dinner, the younger Yang entertained us with stories of Bozhou's potential as a tourist site. The elder Yang said nothing, but gazed absently, oblivious to everyone around him.

The younger Yang and Ding Liang talked and talked, of the development of Bozhou, of foreign investment in the province, of the great future of tourism in China. I listened half-heartedly, my attention wandering from the Arabic calligraphy displayed on the wall to the scent of the spices perfuming the air of the house to the Qur'an and then back to the elder Yang, with his unnerving gaze and his pristine white skullcap.

It was mid-afternoon when the elderly Yang suddenly rose from his chair and began to walk, as if drawn by an unseen force, towards the door. He stopped to pick up a string of white prayer beads, nodded to us all, and slipped out.

Still deeply absorbed in their discussion of tourism in Bozhou, the younger Yang and Ding Liang hardly noticed the elder Yang's absence, but I began to grow restless.

Curious to know where he had gone, I asked the younger Yang during a brief pause between stories.

"My father has gone to the mosque," he said.

"I'd like to go with him," I heard myself saying.

"To the mosque?" the younger Yang repeated in a puzzled but polite voice. Ding Liang looked at me, uncomprehending. Clearly, as far as he had understood it, my claim to be a Muslim was a private joke between the two of us.

"But I would like to take you on a tour of the rest of the city," said Mr. Yang. "I wish you to see the old opera pavilion and the birthplace of Hua Tuo."

"I want to go to the mosque," I insisted, surprising even myself with the conviction behind my words.

"Yes, of course, to the mosque," said Mr. Yang. "I am getting my coat right now." He smiled in an effort to placate me. Working as a tourist guide, I thought, he must have grown used to the whims of foreigners.

Completely perplexed but unquestioning, he reached for his coat. "Shall we go?" He bowed slightly in my direction.

I bowed in return. "Let's go."

It had been barely five minutes since the old man had left. I knew we could catch up with him, since his pace was slow. Before long, we saw his bent form puttering along, step by painstaking step, towards the mosque. We walked beside him. He knew we were there, but he didn't acknowledge our presence. His eyes were fixed on a point straight ahead. It was almost as if he carried us through the force of his own magnetism to his destination. Out of respect for the elder Yang's meditation, we observed silence as we walked.

We penetrated deeper and deeper into the heart of the Muslim section of the city, until the lane swung sharply left. At the end of the lane, a broad stairway beckoned. A few elderly men were climbing the stairs. The elder Yang tottered up them too, flanked on one side by his son and on the other by Ding Liang and me.

I knew that women were often not allowed to enter mosques, and that sometimes they prayed in a separate section. But here, no rules seemed to apply. When I entered the courtyard the chief mullah, a grey-haired man of about sixty, came forward to greet me. We exchanged a few words in Chinese; then the mullah asked me into his study and offered to answer any questions I might have, with Ding Liang serving as my translator.

My eyes scanned the small library of Arabic books. A hundred questions raced through my mind, but no words came. I wanted to ask, for example, "How did you become a mullah? How recently have you resumed your worship? Do you speak Arabic? Could you chant a prayer for me?" I hardly knew where to begin. After several moments had passed, the mullah closed his eyes, folded his hands on his lap, and began to chant. Melodious and penetrating, his voice had the clarity of a very young man's.

Those pure tones in Arabic conjured in my mind worlds of enchantment. I recalled the *1,001 Arabian Nights* of my childhood and the Qur'anic world I had first encountered as a student when, finding myself in an unfamiliar part of the library, I had reached for a book and opened it to the surah describing the Night Journey of the Prophet Muhammad. The chant resonated through my body, transporting me to worlds familiar and unknown. Then, suddenly, it ended, leaving my mind empty of all thoughts and questions.

"Would you like to see the place of prayer?" the mullah asked me. "Would you like to enter the mosque?"

At the threshold of the mosque, we removed our shoes. I covered my head with the scarf I had been wearing around my neck. The elder Yang joined the faithful; the younger Yang, Ding Liang, and I stood near the door.

Standing before their prayer rugs, the men faced away from us, towards Mecca and the Kaaba. The mullah led the men in prayer, intoning some verses in Arabic ending with "Allah-u-Akbar!"

After prayers, the men walked quietly towards the door. Ding Liang and I put on our shoes and left the mosque. Outside, the men greeted one another with nods and smiles. One of them gestured towards me, pointing at my camera. A photo, the finishing touch on any formal gathering in China, was in order. They all tried their best to strike a dignified pose; then the men dispersed and the mullah said goodbye, welcoming us to visit the mosque again anytime we were in Bozhou.

Throughout the long drive home, Ding Liang brooded in silence. When we passed a row of poplar trees lining the road, I pointed to it, trying to make conversation. "Poplar trees lined the backyard of the house where I grew up. At night, I used to imagine they were a choir singing me to sleep." Usually hungry for stories of my Canadian childhood, Ding nodded his head absent-mindedly.

The sun was setting, a great dob of pink paint running down the violet canvas of sky. "Look at the colours!" I exclaimed. But Ding was unreachable.

Two hours passed. It had been dark for some time and I was dozing quietly in the back seat when I was awakened by a voice speaking softly. " 'Allah-u-Akbar,' was it?" Ding asked.

"Yes, I think so."

"It means 'God Is Most Great'?"

"Yes, 'God Is Most Great.' "

Amitabha!

"HOUYCH PITOOEE!" When Lao Zheng disgorged his spittle, I knew it was exactly five thirty. By the time I rose to look out the window, it would be getting light. It was the same every morning: Lao Zheng and Old Liu would stand erect, like two old soldiers, at either end of the guest-house driveway. As dawn broke, one would begin to sweep slowly, methodically with his broom from the east side of the courtyard, while the other swept from the west side of the courtyard until they met just in front of the Chinese garden. There they would stop and greet one another with "Chi fan le ma?" (Have you eaten?), then retire to their separate domains.

Old Liu had a small room in the gatehouse through which the foreign guests had to pass when they returned from outings with friends late at night, meaning anytime past ten o'clock. Lao Zheng had homier quarters: a small room just off the guest-house foyer with the narrowest bed I had ever seen, covered by a threadbare red gingham sheet and fully enclosed in mosquito netting. Beside the bed stood a small wooden washstand with a white metal bowl on top of it. Lao Zheng had strung a clothesline across one corner of the room. Every night he hung on it a freshly hand-washed change of white undershirt, which, together with his blue Mao suit and the undergarments he wore, made up the full extent of his wardrobe.

Lao Zheng also had a sideboard in his room. In the top drawer, he often stored a leg of duck or chicken for his dinner. Like many Chinese, Lao Zheng placed great importance on food—its quality, its quantity, its variety. He broached the subject each mealtime as I walked into the guest-house carrying my mess tin marked No. 68. He was always eager to know what I carried inside my tin, and he sometimes encouraged me to take the lid off to show him the contents, or even to put the mess tin up to his nose so he could smell the food inside and we could discuss its merits or its shortcomings. But it wasn't a one-way street: Lao Zheng offered me his food too, and not just for viewing but for eating. Food was the basis of our friendship. Food and Amitabha (in Chinese, "O-mi-t'o-fo").

Old Liu knew nothing about Amitabha, nor did he care. When I left with the other foreign teachers in the university car for a weekend at Jiuhua Shan, one of China's four holy Buddhist mountains, Old Liu said nothing. But for Lao Zheng the trip was a source of fascination. He must have heard about pilgrimage to such mountains in traditional sayings and in ancient poems, and he would have seen them depicted in Chinese brushstroke paintings. They would have been a prominent and enduring feature of his mental landscape.

For Lao Zheng, the mountain was more than a distant and exotic destination and more than a cultural landmark: it was a place for Amitabha. As I tried in my broken Chinese to explain where I was going, Lao Zheng began to smile, nod, and repeat the word over and over. Amitabha, the name of the great Buddhist saviour; translated into English, it means Infinite Light. It seemed that the old soldier was a Buddhist, and in his broad-minded conception of things he thought I was too. Why else would I nod and say "Amitabha!" in response to his own greeting instead of looking at him blankly as the other foreign teachers did?

When the time came for us to set off for the mountain, Lao Zheng grew very animated. While Old Liu dozed in the gatehouse, Lao Zheng chanted "hao, hao," (good, good) as he shooed us towards the car, his head bobbing up and down with excitement. I turned around as we drove away from the guest-house to catch one last glimpse of Lao Zheng. He was standing in the courtyard, nodding and repeating the holy word *Amitabha*.

It was the beginning of October, the height of autumn in the mountains. In the fields on either side of us, the peasants laboured to harvest the last tea and rice crops of the year. From time to time we passed a brown-robed Buddhist monk approaching the mountain on foot, with only a small satchel in hand. At last we drove into a village at the base of the mountain. The air was cool and a light breeze wafted the odour of austerity everywhere.

Our hotel was called The Gate of Heaven. But the hotel was far from heaven, farther than North America was from China. The showers didn't work. There weren't enough blankets to keep us warm at night. There was no *kaishui* (boiling water) for drinking. Beth, a fellow teacher from the university, complained that her bed was lumpy. I was relieved to escape at dawn for prayers at the temple. On my way, I passed an austere monastery-hostel, where a grandmother had somehow managed to fit her six-year-old grandson into her narrow cot with her.

The Chinese staying there had travelled for miles on this journey of a lifetime to rest their heads at its end on a narrow, metal-framed cot in a dormitory with as many as nineteen others. There was no heat in the monastery, and the mountain nights were already growing cold. Still, the pilgrims laughed amongst themselves after rising from a

29

night of sleeping in their longjohns and clothes. They had brought their food with them: a simple breakfast of bread, pickled vegetables, and tea.

Dawn prayers in the temple consisted of kowtowing, endless chanting, beating gongs, burning incense, and the circumambulation of the holy precincts by a head monk dressed in elaborate red and saffron-coloured robes. Various assistants followed him, then fellow devotees all the way down to the novices, who with their shaved heads and quizzical round eyes looked more like curious schoolboys than initiates into the spiritual mysteries of the Sutras. The ceremony, it seemed, was as much for show as for devotion. Still, I marvelled at how the Buddhist scriptures, carried on foot to China many centuries ago, had taken root in this foreign soil and produced a unique hybrid, a rare but hardy vine fully adapted to the cool, thin air of these mountains.

When the ceremony had ended, I walked around to the back of the shrine, where I discovered a statue of Guanyin. I remembered when I had first seen her standing benignly on the family altar of every home in a small fishing village in southern China, how she had glowed out from the doorways, enthroned by the light of a host of red electic candles and sentinelled by a few surrounding sticks of incense. Guanyin, goddess of mercy, the female face of Buddhism, queen of hearts—I kowtowed before her several times as a gesture of good faith before setting out to climb the holy mountain.

We spent the whole autumn day hiking up Jiuhua Shan. Dan and I made it up the thousands of steps to the top. On the way, we passed a bamboo forest, with its thin stalks in a dense array of sharply pointed, delicate leaves, each one plucked as if from a Chinese brushstroke painting. We also passed numerous shrines to the Buddha, where we felt compelled to divest ourselves of our worldly attachments—a few Chinese *jiao* (fifty-cent note) with vignettes of life in the New China on either side.

Near one of these shrines, I met an elderly Buddhist nun with a shaved head and lily feet, sitting with a cane in her hand on top of a low wall adjacent to the pilgrim path. Farther up the mountain, I passed another elderly devotee, a pilgrim, who kissed each step as she climbed, pausing at each one to utter the holy word *Amitabha!*

The higher up the mountain we climbed the more derelict grew the monasteries. In one, I found an old monk sleeping on the floor of the temple. Another monastery smelt powerfully of mildew and decaying wood, and the images of the Buddha were chipped and broken, with their paint peeling off. At the peak of the mountain, the light broke through the clouds as we celebrated the end of our journey with a group of students from Nanjing.

The students drew us into their laughter and their triumph by taking photos of us all in front of the monastery at the top of the mountain. Dan and I left our tribute there too, as a final, symbolic gesture of detachment from our worldly desires. I recall buying a candle with my few remaining Chinese *jiao* and carrying it through the rooms of this upper mansion.

When I returned, it was impossible for me to tell Lao Zheng what impression the trip had made on me. We had no common language. But the way he rushed towards me with greetings and nods, and gazed at me, eyes shining, as I stepped out of the car, told me that he understood something, perhaps everything, of the significance of my journey. The next day, when I walked past his room carrying my mess tin, his eyes lit up. He smiled at me and spoke slowly but excitedly, as if to a child: "Jiuhua Shan hen da!" (The holy mountain is very big!). I nodded my head in agreement. Fortunately, it was a theme that required no further discussion.

The day after I returned from the holy mountain, I was invited by one of my night-school students to visit the new nightclub in town. I accepted, not because I liked nightclubs, but because Hong Liu was so eager to show me the glories of modern Hefei. The nightclub was suitably equipped with strobe lights, a dance floor, and a fine team of break-dancers. Periodically, more sophisticated dancers took the floor, swaying through a waltz, striding through a tango, and marching through a group step-dance the Chinese youth loved to do *en masse*.

As Hong Liu and I rode home in the moonlight, our bicycles whirred with the excitement of forbidden pleasure. It was eleven o'clock, by guest-house standards very late. To enter the guest-house, we would need not just tact, but a strategy of attack. All the gates and doors would be solidly locked.

First, we penetrated the university gates, identifying ourselves and explaining to the sentinel posted there why we were out so late. Next, I had to creep through the gatehouse, where Old Liu lived. The door was shut fast for the night. Old Liu was snoring like a dragon in his lair, guarding his precious jewel, the guest-house. Hong Liu and I knocked softly at first, then louder and louder. Finally, we heard a voice call out: "Bu zai!" We knocked again, this time more insistently. The same reply: "Bu zai!"

In response, Hong Liu spoke rapidly in Chinese. Old Liu called out again, "Bu zai!" This time when Hong Liu answered, I heard the words *waiguo ren* (foreigner). "Lao wai!" (Outlander!), Old Liu muttered, using a not very flattering term for "foreigner," and opened the door. Hong Liu and I didn't even take time to say good night. I crept through the gatehouse as quietly as I could with my rickety old bicycle in my grip, whispering "Duibuqi! Duibuqi!" (Sorry! Sorry!). Old Liu pulled himself up from the bed and sat on its edge in his long underwear, hunched over with the heaviness of sleep. He didn't watch me go by, but concentrated instead on lighting a cigarette. I stood inside the guest-house courtyard now. Home free! Now I had to storm the bastion itself, with the help of Lao Zheng.

I crept quietly through the courtyard, steering my bicycle past the Chinese garden. Outside the guest-house, I propped it on its kickstand and locked it with my key. The doors were bound with a heavy iron chain. It was well past eleven o'clock now. Lao Zheng no longer sat with the other guest-house staff in a semicircle watching the television that Ye Ye had appropriated from one of the empty rooms for the viewing pleasure of the staff when business was slow, which was most of the time. Since no lights were on in the foyer, I assumed Lao Zheng was sleeping in his cot in the back room.

I crept around to the back of the guest-house and tapped lightly on Lao Zheng's window. Instantly, he was awake. Like the five wise virgins in the Bible who trimmed their lamps in expectation of the bridegroom, Lao Zheng always seemed to be waiting for a call, even if it was just a call from me to open the door. Before I could circle back around to the front of the guest-house, the chains were hanging slack and the door stood open, inviting me in to my cosy bed. Behind the door Lao Zheng stood, motioning me to enter, nodding his head, and smiling with his Buddha eyes closed. As I made my way to my room, I whispered my thanks to the old soldier, who answered me in Chinese, insisting that it was "nothing, nothing at all."

To make up for the inconvenience I had caused him, the next day I had a student translate for Lao Zheng my story of the evening, with Old Liu's cry "Bu zai!" as its climax. Hong Liu had already explained to me that *bu zai* meant "not home." As he listened, Lao Zheng smiled forgivingly then grew serious. "Bu zai," he said in Chinese, picking up on the final word of my narrative, "has another meaning as well." He closed his eyes, stiffened his arms, and leaned back, wiping all expression from his face.

I looked at my translator, Miss Qu. Her eyes darted away from mine in embarrassment. She spoke in a low voice. "Teacher, I don't know how to tell you this, but if you add a 'le,' bu zai can also mean *dead!*" She finished with relief. Lao Zheng's lips broke into a broad, irrepressible smile. He laughed with a deep, throaty laugh until he

began to cough violently, because he chain-smoked cigarettes and because the air was filled with coal dust and he
had been breathing it all his life. Then he smiled and
asked, "Chi fan le ma?"

Not long afterwards, changes of the utmost significance took place in the guest-house courtyard. First, we
heard the banging of boards being nailed together. The
next thing we knew Old Liu had a new gatehouse. It was
considerably larger than the previous gatehouse, with two
rooms instead of one: a bedroom in the inner sanctum and
a transit room, through which foreign guests and visitors
had to pass on their way to the guest-house. The old gatehouse stood by the gate near the pond where the campus
workers fished in the early morning and the students harvested fresh water chestnuts during the Mid-autumn
Festival. But the new gatehouse looked enterprisingly eastward out onto Anyi Lu, the road leading to the city.

To all who came within its ambience, the new gatehouse seemed to mean business. It was felt that its estab-
lishment raised the guest-house to a new and higher level.
Now Old Liu could be found sitting on the stoop of the
gatehouse looking out with an air of condescension on the
street below, where an occasional stroller and an even
more occasional bicyclist gave life to the static scene.

The new gatehouse seemed to mean business, but, in
reality, the effectiveness of the gatehouse had declined.
Now we came and went easily through the transit room as
Old Liu dozed peacefully in the inner sanctum. As for Lao
Zheng, he didn't think much one way or the other about
the new gatehouse, but rested content with a duck leg
stored in his sideboard.

When I left China in June 1989, in the wake of the
Tiananmen tragedy, Lao Zheng came out of the foyer with
the other guest-house staff to see me off. That noon I
tramped, one last time, to the teachers' cafeteria, to trade
my rice and vegetable tickets for a hot, delicious meal. The
campus was quiet and tense with the crackdown, and not a

child's voice or even a cat's meow could be heard any-where. No one dared even to listen to the radio for fear that his choice of station might be interpreted in a politi-cal light.

When I returned from the teachers' cafeteria, Lao Zheng asked one last time about my food. One last time I lifted the mess tin numbered 68 to his nose. Our covenant was fulfilled: I had given Lao Zheng the vicarious pleasure of pilgrimage to a holy place and he had seen me through a whole year of cafeteria meals. He must have been a good cook, I speculated; he had certainly been an excellent critic.

The foreign teachers were leaving in pairs. The day before, Bob and Beth had left. Now Dan and I were being driven to the airport. Many people came to see us off on that last day. I remember Mrs. Li, a young mother full of ambition for herself and her child, breaking into tears as I walked down the red-carpeted hall one last time. Now she would have no one with whom to practise her English. I also remember the solemn faces of my graduate students of Shakespeare and the dean's speech about how sad he was that we had to leave in this way. But most of all, I remember the bobbing head of Lao Zheng, his half-closed Buddha eyes sparkling from behind their slanted lids as he smiled, nodded, and uttered one last "Amitabha!" when the car pulled away from the guest-house.

Before I knew it, a year in Canada had passed. Already an urban spring flaunted its green twigs of life, its gay sprouts shocking the grey city blocks. I celebrated the first hyacinths and took long walks at night in the light spring rain, but still, I missed the orchards at Dashu Shan and my *ba-jiao* grove and the Chinese garden framing it. The trees in the grove would just then be putting out their first green shoots into the world, I remembered. Memories kept stir-ring, drawing me back. I decided to book a ticket to China.

I arrived at the guest-house exactly one year after my departure. The whole campus slept, sunk in the deep, humid dream that is summer in Hefei. The students had gone home. But Old Liu still sat on his chair, sphinx-like, immovable, looking on the passing scene with a detachment amounting to disdain. He barely moved as we exchanged greetings. As I passed through the gatehouse, I wondered if Old Liu and Lao Zheng still laboured at dawn to sweep the guest-house driveway, meeting in front of the Chinese garden to exchange greetings.

I entered the guest-house and stood for a minute in the foyer, where Lao Zheng usually sat in his chair watching TV or drinking a cup of tea. I looked down the hall and inside the dining room. Not a sign of life. Then Chen came swishing towards me, mop in hand, and greeted me. Chen, Ye Ye, and Zhong Mei—all seemed glad to see me. I don't think any of them remembered how grumpy I could be when they came unannounced into my room at eight o'clock on Saturday mornings to change the bedclothes. We talked a little. My Chinese had improved considerably during the year I had lived in the guest-house and again during the subsequent year in Canada, where I had taken classes in Mandarin at the university. Now we met as comrades and friends who spoke something of the same language.

I asked after everyone we knew in common, and we laughingly remembered various highlights of my year in the guest-house. But the whole time, I couldn't stop wondering: where was Lao Zheng? When I saw they weren't going to volunteer the information, I asked: "Lao Zheng, zai nar?" (Lao Zheng, where is he?).

Chen, Ye Ye, and Zhong Mei looked at me serenely. "Lao Zheng," Chen said so softly I could hardly make out her words, "Lao Zheng bu zai. . . ."

"Bu zai . . . bu zai . . . ," I repeated, meditating on the meaning of the word. "Hao, hao, hao. . . ."

I could have asked but I did not want to know whether Lao Zheng had gone back to his home town for a visit with his family, or whether he had just gone out shopping for vegetables. I did not want to know whether he had left the guest-house for some heavenly mansion above, where surely there would be a room of adequate size for him and a daily cuisine that was truly divine. As I left the guest-house, I passed by his room quickly, not looking in to see if his possessions had been removed.

As I walked towards the gatehouse, the eyes of the guest-house seemed to follow me. Chen, Ye Ye, and Zhong Mei peered out from behind the glass doors and waved. The courtyard itself was empty. No one stood quietly nodding or smiling. No soul extended a simple gesture of friendship. I was about to step into Old Liu's gatehouse and leave the guest-house behind me, possibly forever, when suddenly I felt compelled to turn around.

As I turned my head quickly, my eyes must have played a trick on me. I thought I saw a bent and stocky figure clad in a blue Mao jacket, head bobbing up and down, and brown, slanted Buddha eyes glimmering in the sunlight. I thought I heard a single word resound through the empty space of the courtyard, and I thought that word was *Amitabha!*

The Utterance

MR. TAN SAT GUARDING the entrance of the Foreign Guest-house, with pen in hand, in the same spirit that the archangel Michael must have brandished his flaming sword as he stood before the gates of paradise. Mr. Tan was the main clerk on staff at the guest-house. His job was to register visitors who came to see the foreign teachers. But his mission was to keep out undesirables.

It was an easy mission. Two large doors opened onto a back courtyard, but these were always chained shut. Beyond the doors loomed a tall, iron-grated fence, with gates also perpetually locked. In any season, only light could come streaming through the back door, and in the spring it made luminous the magnolia trees in the Chinese garden and set the cherry trees into brilliant pink flame. Even the front doors posed only a small challenge, since visitors trickled through at the rate of five or six a day.

Except in the evening, when the staff gathered to watch TV, the foyer of the guest-house was a quiet, airy place. There, under the flickering light cast by fluttering tree shadows, Mr. Tan studied his English. Absorbed for hours, his exercise books spread before him, he remained oblivious to everyone who came and went. He read any English literature he could find: simple readers from English night-school courses and even grammar books filled with methodical exercises, which he painstakingly practised over and over again.

Most of all, Mr. Tan loved to study the English-language *China Daily*. It didn't take long for me to figure out why the *China Daily* appeared only twice, at most three times, a week. Mr. Tan had his own plans for the paper. At noon, as all the guest-house slept, Mr. Tan recited aloud article after article. Once I corrected his pronunciation as he read aloud a feature article on Canada's political system.

Mr. Tan was much more than a guest-house sentry: he sat with his pen balanced over the visitors' daybook as if he were about to write something profound, perhaps a book of philosophy or even a novel. Mr. Tan told me he had taken the job solely to practise his English. English, he declared, was his only hope. So he spent his time bent over old issues of the newspaper, rooting out unfamiliar words and underlining them, then writing the definitions in Chinese characters in the margin.

I don't think Mr. Tan's English improved one bit the whole year I lived in Room 202 of the Foreign Guest-house, but our friendship did grow, especially after Mr. Tan's emotional crisis. One day when I returned from classes, Mr. Tan's big moon-shaped eyes drooped more than usual. It seemed as if—as much as is possible for a Chinese man— he was on the verge of crying in public.

"What's wrong?" I asked, alarmed.

"Can you tell I'm upset?"

"Yes."

He answered ruefully, his eyes filling up with tears: "I was criticized by my leader this morning." Mr. Tan told me that he had risen before dawn to buy a ticket for a foreign guest, but had returned from the train station empty-handed. His eyes began to water again, and tears rolled down his cheeks.

"Never mind," I said. "Your leader's being unfair."

By the end of our chat, Mr. Tan was smiling. "You know, in China," he said, "when a man has a friendship with a woman older than him, he calls her jie jie—in Chinese, means 'big sister.' I can call you that?"

It didn't matter that I was only one year older than Mr. Tan. "I'd like that," I replied.

Galvanized by his success at winning my friendship, Mr. Tan grew bold. "I know you foreigners like to go to church. May sometime I accompany you?"

I was not in the habit of visiting the local church, but I couldn't disappoint Mr. Tan. "Of course," I said. When it came to finding opportunities to practise English, Mr. Tan's ingenuity was boundless.

The next Sunday Mr. Tan came whirling through the gates of the guest-house. "Duibuqi! Duibuqi!" he cried. "So sorry I am late! I am ready now."

"No matter," I answered in my newly acquired Chinglish. "Let's go!"

Mr. Tan cycled on the outside, to protect me from reckless drivers, he explained. It took us twenty minutes to cycle to the church. When we arrived, the service was just beginning. "Yesu ling wo!" (Jesus leads me), wailed the dense crowd of peasants and workers lining the narrow alleyway that led to the rear door of the church.

We pushed through the crowded back room, where loudspeakers blared out the service for those who couldn't fit inside the church. Elderly women and men dressed in blue cotton Mao jackets sat at desks in what looked like a large classroom, their noses pressed close to open Bibles. When Pastor Fu and his wife saw that a foreigner was coming, they pushed aside the crowds to make way for me. Embarrassed, I wove my way through the masses of people with Mr. Tan in tow. Toothless women with wide grins nodded at me as I passed.

Pastor Fu led us past the flock of singing angels dressed in white linen smocks to an empty space in the foreigners' pews, the first two in the church. A peasant woman also followed Pastor Fu, making her way through the crowds in the wake of his passing just as the Israelites must have rushed after Moses when he parted the Red Sea. The woman carried her Sunday dinner, a live chicken, in her hand. When Pastor Fu saw the chicken, he cornered her and asked her to leave the chicken outside. But she broke free just by the angel-choir and scrambled up the stairs, disappearing into the packed recesses of the church.

The wooden floorboards creaked under their burden, as in a crowded ark. Women and children lined each stair. Peasant women crouched on wooden stools, vying for every available inch of floor space. Behind me, an elderly woman, faced lined by years of hard labour in the elements, wrung her hands and wept loudly, her tears forming a bitter pool on the floor beneath her.

I could barely hear the preacher, a young woman with a radiant complexion whose head tilted naturally heavenward as she spoke. The friend of the hysterical woman uttered an occasional moan, as if to show solidarity with her companion. But when I turned around to glance at them, they smiled and nodded their heads rapidly, like apples bobbing in a pail of water. Hysteria, it seemed, was just their way of showing sincerity. After all, this was a Protestant church established by evangelists in the early twentieth century. The missionaries had done their work well.

But Mr. Tan heard neither the sermon nor the weeping. His mind was completely absorbed in an English Bible some well-meaning foreigner had passed his way. I knew I had lost him. Transported by the Word, in English, he had entered the Kingdom of Names. After a few minutes, Mr. Tan awakened from his trance to his mission in the church: to translate the sermon for me.

The Chinese was beyond his knowledge of English

41

equivalents, so he spent most of his time thumbing through his Chinese-English dictionary for the swiftly passing words that flowed by as rapidly as the river of life itself. Mr. Tan looked like someone about to drown. He would sink and then surface again, fighting to keep afloat in a sea of English in which words shunted up against one another like ships trying to put into port in a small and crowded harbour.

"What is the church?" Mr. Tan began to translate. "The church is not just a building. The church is a people. It is a path. . . ."

When the sermon was over, the radiant young angel, obviously a minister in training, stepped down from the pulpit. Pastor Fu stepped forward. It was Easter and time for breaking bread and drinking wine in the holy communion of the Lord.

"All those who are Christians, please stand!" Pastor Fu cried out in a tone curiously militaristic. "All those who are baptized believers," he called out, "raise your right hand!"

Most of the people in the pews stood up and raised their hands. Mr. Tan looked up at me, puzzled. I motioned him to stand. He looked at me again with a ghostly look, his eyes filled with doubt and apprehension. The thin veil of self-assurance behind which he usually hid had been torn away, leaving him completely vulnerable. Madame Wong approached us with the wine and the bread. She handed the bread graciously to me, then passed it on suspiciously to Mr. Tan. Instinctively, he quivered and shrank back as her hand touched his. Then he forced himself to open his hand and receive the crumb. As he did, a torrent of words poured from Madame Wong's lips. "Are you a Christian? Have you been baptized?" she began her interrogation. Mr. Tan stumbled to find the correct answers. "Are you a church member? Do you believe in our Lord?" she persisted. "Have you been saved?"

Struck dumb with fear and shame, Mr. Tan let the

words come at him as if he had been called upon to suffer martyrdom at the hands of Madame Wong for a cause that had something to do—he vaguely understood—with the small, block-like print, the English words in the precious book he held in his hands.

I leaned protectively towards Mr. Tan and answered Madame Wong, "Yes! Yes! To all your questions, yes!"

Madame Wong looked at Mr. Tan and then back at me. Her glance took in the small leather-bound volume Mr. Tan clasped in his hands. As she passed him a small cup of wine, she whispered something in his ear. Mr. Tan looked terrified. He could hardly swallow the bread and choked a little on the wine. I held his hand as the congregation recited the Lord's Prayer.

Mr. Tan stumbled along, mouthing the words as if reciting a mantra to calm himself. He sighed with relief when the prayer was over and took his seat again, never once loosening his hold on the leather-bound book.

After the closing hymn, the faithful rushed for the door, each vying to be the first out. It was not that they especially wanted to get out, just that they wanted, as all sinners do, to be first. Mr. Tan and I sat in the pew and waited for the crowds to disperse. He was still lost in meditation on the Word. The black, leather-bound book remained open and he seemed to be floating, buoyed up once again by the English words. I glanced over at the open pages. Mr. Tan's finger moved along beneath these lines: "Except ye be converted, and become as little children, ye shall not enter into the kingdom of heaven. . . ." Mr. Tan turned to me, his eyes filled with amazement.

The church was practically empty now. Among the last stragglers, a woman with short grey hair and a wizened face hobbled towards the altar and kowtowed as she laid some red paper money before it. A group of peasant women stood in a circle near the chancel, intoning verses and laying hands on another peasant woman who moaned and writhed in their midst.

Mr. Tan turned to me, incredulous. He asked, "Are you a Christian?" As I considered how to answer, the peasant woman at the centre of the circle suddenly stopped moaning. The atoms in the pew where Mr. Tan and I sat seemed to vibrate with the sound as the woman uttered a sharp, clear cry: "Alleluia!"

Where the Yangtze Meets the Ganges River

I CAME CARRYING an olive branch, or, more accurately, a dried, dusty, but perfectly shaped poplar leaf that I had picked up and pressed in a notebook after a morning walk on the university campus. I had been invited to India in January, during the Spring Festival vacation, to give lectures on Canadian literature. I carried the leaf as a token of new friendships in China, and as a reminder of the Chinese New Year, which I would miss while in India. I did not expect that on the eve of the Chinese New Year I would be walking down a dark highway from Allahabad to join the largest gathering of human beings ever on the face of the earth, congregated to celebrate the holy festival of the *kumbh*.

This was an especially auspicious celebration, I was told, since the sun, stars, and moon were in a rare alignment that would not occur again for another seventy-two years. Fifteen million people from all over India had temporarily migrated to the *sangam*, the confluence of the Ganges and Yamuna Rivers, for the holy dip, a ritual of

45

purification believed to wash away sins and guarantee ever-lasting life. Whole villages moved together, connected only by a fragile string. Children clung to the saris of their mothers, and women to the scarves of their husbands. Mamaji was my protector. The cousin-by-marriage of a Canadian friend whose husband was a Sharma from Lucknow, Mamaji descended from a long line of princes. When the Republic of India was formed, his kingdom had been relegated to oblivion. Now Mamaji was only a villager, but he walked with an aristocratic gait as he led the way down the dark highway.

We reached the holy Ganges just before dawn. A procession of sadhus, or holy men, passed by, their long hair tangled with flowers soaked in Ganges' water. As dawn broke, the chanting of the Hare Krishna grew louder. The light revealed a vast mosaic of brightly coloured saris stretching for miles on either side of the river. An elderly woman, dressed in white, sprang forward, moving in joyous contortions towards the river bank, singing and clapping. Now the crowd pressed hard. To the right, a group of young men playfully incited it to stampede towards the water. Mamaji took firm control, appointing a small band of pilgrims from his village to walk in a circle around me, one in front, one behind, and one to hold onto each of my trembling hands. Then he crooked his finger and led us in the opposite direction.

On the other side of the river we found a clear, safe place. We set down our belongings, a woman from Mamaji's village and me staying behind to mark the spot while the men set off to the river. Then we were to take our turn. I spoke no Hindi, so I could not explain to Mamaji that I wouldn't be able to take the holy dip. I had just recovered from bronchitis, and I didn't think my fragile immune system could withstand the impurities of the water. But when I waved my hand in refusal, Mamaji simply sprinkled me with the water still dripping from his hands. It was cool but refreshing.

At least I could throw some flowers in the river, I thought. I saw red roses rippling in the water and golden marigolds floating downstream, flickering like small patches of the rising sun. Now the sun rose, a huge pink ball peeping over the massive tent village, home to millions of pilgrims. But I could see no flower vendors on this side of the river. I felt in my purse for my notebook and looked through it for the dusty leaf. Then I gave the leaf to Mamaji, asking him, through pantomime gestures, to set the leaf afloat downstream with a blessing and a prayer.

The morning grew luminous as Mamaji waded out into the holy Ganges. The millions flooding the banks and shallow waters came more and more sharply into focus. For a moment, I could barely identify Mamaji; as he walked towards the sun, he became just another radiant silhouette. Then he dipped like a fish into the cold waters, disappearing entirely from sight. Suddenly he emerged, splashing and joyous. No leaf was in his hand as he raised it to wave to me. It was hard to see against the glare of the rising sun, but I thought I saw him watching the no-longer-dusty leaf swirling its way downstream, twirling in the eddies of the current.

When I returned to China, my students eagerly asked about my journey. What had I seen? What had I done? What were the people of India like? I described my pilgrimage to the Ganges. Then I told them about the poplar leaf I had found on campus and set afloat in the river during the festival of the holy *kumbh*. They sat for a minute in thoughtful silence. After I dismissed the class, one young woman lingered behind with a question.

"Is it really a holy festival?" she asked me.

"For the Hindus it is."

"Then thank you, Teacher, I mean for the leaf."

I wondered if Mamaji's prayer had already been answered.

IN THE EYE OF THE STORM

Yu Lan would never forget my words, and I would never forget that last ride to the airport with her. The rice paddies sparkled, emerald in the morning light. It did not seem that we were caught up in one of the most tragic political incidents in China's recent history. It seemed that all was well. I said to Yu Lan, "We are travelling in the eye of a storm."

An unearthly calm held the countryside in its grip. We moved in a surreal world of dreams, our minds numbed by shock. Only days before we had heard that as many as a thousand students and civilians had lost their lives in Tiananmen Square. It was my first contact ever with social violence, and the effect on me was greater than I could ever have imagined.

I realized I had romanticized those epoch-making episodes and incidents that had changed the face of modern China, of Europe, and of the former Soviet Union. I saw etched beneath the bold design that social movements paint on the canvas of history the daily struggles of ordinary people, people who needed to buy rice and vegetables, who had a bicycle to fix or an aging parent to care for.

It was in the lives of ordinary people that the political events registered most profoundly. For example, Wu Li might not be able to join her husband in America. Wu Hong would not be allowed to pursue graduate studies until she had worked for several years. The Chinese mourned not only the death of the students, but the death of their dreams.

Yet, paradoxically, everyday life triumphed in the end, remaining somehow unaffected by the catastrophe. Life went on, regardless of what had touched it—violence, death, despair. I found this dogged persistence at the business of life one of the most remarkable qualities of the Chinese spirit; it seemed to be rooted in an incredible resilience that dictated adaptation to and acceptance of whatever is. I couldn't help but remember the words of Lao Tsu:

> A tree that is unbending is easily broken.
> The hard and strong will fall.
> The soft and weak will overcome.

In November 1992, I flew on one of the first direct flights to Beijing from Tel Aviv, over the Gobi Desert. It was a new approach, both geographically and psychologically. When I touched down in Beijing, I sensed that the trauma of those spring 1989 days had finally begun to fade. Especially in Shanghai, a burgeoning spirit of optimism seemed to surge up from the very pavement of the streets. Business boomed, transforming the city into a vast construction site. The lesson was simple: the Chinese people had endured. History had been their greatest teacher.

China Spring, 1989

ONE THING I LEARNED in China: revolution is searingly personal. Before China, the word *revolution* conjured in my mind visions of epic struggles
between the forces of light and darkness featuring larger-than-life players: the stormy firebrands of the Paris Commune, the stalwart heroes of the Russian Revolution, the feisty comrades of the Long March. But living inside a revolution, you see its human face and learn that it is ordinary, terrifyingly mundane, with a way of weaving itself into the fabric of everyday life.

Inside China, no media images portrayed the cataclysmic events that shook the country, their impact radiating outwards from the epicentres of power into all facets of our lives. In what seemed to be a concession to the students' demands for a freer press, there were, at least in the early days of the struggle, a couple of shots of Tiananmen Square on the state-controlled China Central Television. Once we even saw foreign journalists with placards in the square, campaigning with the students for more freedom of the press. But for the most part, we had to form our own images of the student movement.

April 15—the day Hu Yaobang died—seemed an ordinary day, not the beginning of a revolution. In Hefei, the peasants rose at dawn as usual to haul their home-grown produce to Zhong Caishi, the large vegetable market at the centre of the city. In Beijing, the students responded immediately to Hu's death with eulogies, poems, and essays, and by placing paper wreaths in Tiananmen Square. Two days later, in Hefei, the first student marches took place. About one o'clock in the morning, I was awakened by the roar of a crowd somewhere outside the Foreign Guest-house and by the persistent beat of a drum. In the eerie darkness of the early morning hours, students gathered and called others to assemble in the basketball court outside the Number Three Dining Hall. Before long, many of the students had set off on a march downtown to the Communist Party headquarters.

The movement had begun under the cover of darkness. In the unnatural glare emanating from the single, powerful light bulb that lit the basketball court, few faces could be identified. No one was willing to come forth. The next day I saw my first *dazibao*, large wall posters commonly used in China to convey a political message. And in front of the school shop, a cloth banner hung from the trees. It read "Freedom and Democracy." Quickly, all the posters were torn down by university officials and the cloth banner unstrung. Tense and restless, the students began to skip or, as they put it, "boycott" classes.

Cao Meihua, my best girl student, remarked with disdain, "Some people just want to make a noise. In China, we need some form of stimulation."

On Saturday, April 22, we watched the televised funeral service for Hu Yaobang. All around the city, the red flag of China flew at half-mast. People wore black armbands. Some cried in the streets. The teachers at my university were told by the Party secretary to watch the funeral service as part of their weekly Political Study class.

"Hu," a young teacher named Xu explained, "was the wrong person to die. In China, intellectuals have few friends, but Hu was one of them. Some say Hu's body should rest beside Mao's, but that's impossible. Others joke that Mao's body will have to be strapped down, so he won't rise up to cheer the students on!"

Hu, the former General Secretary of the Chinese Communist Party, had been blamed for a series of student demonstrations that had flared up in Beijing, Hefei, and other cities, Xu explained. He had been forced to resign in January 1987. His moderate response to the fledgling student movement had brought accusations of support for "bourgeois liberalization" from China's top leaders, but won him favour in the eyes of Chinese students and intellectuals. Now, it seemed, his death supplied the tinder to spark the widespread dissatisfaction on university campuses across the country into student protests.

The following Thursday, I flew to Beijing for a job interview at one of the city's leading universities. There I met Qing Hong—in English, "Celebrate Red." Twenty-three years old, she was born, she told me, only hours after the Cultural Revolution broke out. She was tired but exhilarated from the previous night's march to Tiananmen Square, her first-ever march of protest. As we strolled around the grounds of the Summer Palace, she shared her thoughts with me. "Yesterday was the happiest day of my life. For the first time, I felt I was living not just for myself, but for something outside of myself, something bigger than us all."

Qing Hong's words transported us both. We looked at the Fragrant Hills in the distance. I thought about May Fourth, only a few days off. Then I thought about Qing Hong. I couldn't help feeling happy that she had found something to believe in.

On May 2 I travelled on the night train from Beijing to Hefei. I shared my compartment with a middle-aged man. As he said goodbye to his wife at the station, he wept openly. She clung to his hand through the window as the train pulled away. After some time, we began to talk.

"We have been separated for sixteen years," he explained. The man was, it turned out, a professor at my university who had been "sent down" to Hefei during the Cultural Revolution. His wife had remained in Beijing at a government job. Later on, as he slept, I lay on my berth in the darkened cabin, looking at the stars. Bright and penetrating, they burned themselves into my dreams. I lay tossing and turning as I reviewed Professor Wong's story: how he had been forced to bow down before the portrait of Chairman Mao as a kind of penance for his rightist thinking. But worst of all, he had said, was the psychological isolation. To be "capped" meant you'd be isolated, even from those closest to you, for years. "When I think of that time," he had told me, "I weep and laugh. I weep because of the unnecessary suffering, and I laugh because of the nonsense people followed."

May 4. University officials arranged the biggest dance party ever held on campus. There was an indoor dance, with waltzes, tangos, and the rumba; and an outdoor dance, with disco, rock, and Madonna. For the Chinese teachers, attendance was compulsory. Everyone danced the night away. No one had time to think about May Fourth, the day when, in 1919, student demonstrations signalled the beginning of a new, socialist culture in China. The officials were on a roll: they planned a dance for every night of the week. But on Sunday the game was up. Crashers, called by the teachers "bad elements," disrupted the dance. For a moment, the fear of some kind of violence rippled through the throng of dancing couples. The tape stopped abruptly in the middle of a waltz, the lights flashed on, and everybody filed rapidly out of the building and walked home.

That week I taught my last classes of the year. By May 18, the political situation affected everybody. The teachers conferred all night and decided to throw their lot in with the students. The next morning they cabled Beijing announcing their support for the student movement. Classes were officially cancelled until further notice. Ironically, the subject of my last lecture was Ernest Jones's "The Song of the Future," a piece of proletarian poetry all about how to make revolution. It had been difficult to concentrate. Outside the window, a procession of students, drums in hand, called other students to come out of the classrooms into the open air. Some hung out of the classroom windows cheering them on. Others rushed down the stairs and out of the building. Still, I insisted on finishing the class.

"What would you like to talk about?" I asked the remaining students. "History? Literature? Anything but politics."

"Tell us about the Prague Spring," they replied, invoking the memory of that fateful spring in 1968 when another set of students had confronted authority, clashing with invading Soviet tanks in the city of Prague, Czechoslovakia.

That night a rally took place in the school auditorium. Over two thousand students came to hear young teachers analyze the current situation and outline a program for action. It surprised me to discover which of my students were the committed ones. While some slipped off to a dance being held the same night, Miss Bai and her boyfriend, Zhang, waited outside the auditorium for me. At first, students and teachers greeted the speeches with moderate applause. Many, like myself, listened purely out of an interest in the history the student movement was making. The situation had not yet gotten to a point where only the committed ones dared to identify openly with it. For the time being, revolution remained a tempest in the campus teapot.

The speeches lasted for hours. Miss Bai served as my translator. The provincial government had scheduled a televised dialogue with the student leaders for the same night. Staid and repetitive, the television debate generated

Sandra Hutchison

little excitement. But as the evening progressed, the atmosphere in the auditorium grew electric. Students raised their fists in support of a resolution to back the hunger strikers in Beijing. The call for Deng's resignation brought frenzied clapping and standing ovations. Though by any standard a frail, inhibited girl, Miss Bai radiated the strength of her purpose. As she sat on the edge of her chair, face flushed with passion, her boyfriend, Zhang, watched her entranced. One after another, the teachers stepped into the bright spotlight of centre stage. The movement was coming out of the darkness into the light.

Before long, the news reached me that my students were rushing to Beijing. Those on the first trains to the capital collected money from sympathetic crowds to pay for their fares. Soon, passage on all trains to Beijing was declared free of charge for student travellers who wished to lend their support to the protesters in Tiananmen Square. Wu Hong, the most courageous of my girl students, was the first to return from Tiananmen with news.

"By day," she told me, "I slept at the aerospace institute and by night I was a student policeman. But mostly we just sat there. Some of us went for tourist reasons. Really, we should have done more to help the suffering students of Beijing."

Meanwhile, in the central square in Hefei, Miss Li's boyfriend struggled through the third day of a hunger strike that a growing number of students were staging in front of the Communist Party headquarters. Miss Li was constantly in tears, so her roommates elected Miss Pang to go down and check on Miss Li's boyfriend. Since bus service had come to a halt, Miss Pang set out on foot for the centre of the city. Upon arrival, she pushed herself through the charmed circle of hunger strikers only to be rebuffed by Miss Li's boyfriend, who told her that it was no time to think about love, only about revolution. Even Miss Pang's much modified description of the encounter sent Miss Li into fresh torrents of tears until, galvanized by his

56

commitment, she decided to join her boyfriend. Sporting white headbands, boyfriend and girlfriend sat side by side in the city square.

No one was prepared for the imposition of martial law at 10:00 a.m. on May 20. A friend called from Beijing to say that helicopters were flying overhead and troops were moving into the city. We listened in disbelief as Li Peng's hard-line speech played over and over on China Central Television: "The fate and future of the People's Republic of China, built by many revolutionary martyrs with their blood, faces a serious threat. . . ."

Afraid, two of my students took refuge in my room. All they wanted was a quiet place to study. In the media blackout that followed, we listened to the BBC (British Broadcasting Corporation) and the VOA (Voice of America) on my shortwave radio. We spent the day together and the night too. While the city, tense with expectation and fear, braced itself, we burned incense, ate strawberries, listened to Chopin, and read the sonnets of Shakespeare. My two Chinese daughters, as I called them, slept end to end in my spare bed. Each had a chair for her own belongings, simply arranged and neatly folded. That night we felt safe, perhaps because we really couldn't believe the truth. As the sun set, we lit candles against the dark.

Shanghai, the week of May 22, burst with energy. Students congregated day and night on the Bund. The carnival atmosphere of Hefei's demonstrations was a long way from the tense determination of the Shanghai students. In Hefei, the girls wore their best dresses and walked hand in hand, gaily twirling red flags, while the famished boys from the agricultural institute, at least in the early days of the movement, shouted, along with their cries for more democracy, such apolitical slogans as "We want nutrition!" But in Shanghai, the students grew more militant with each passing day.

I visited a colleague at Jiaotong University. "Do you have any pictures of the demonstrations?" he asked. "No,"

I answered and, in an effort to compensate, added, "but would you like one of yourself over there?" I pointed to a nearby garden. It happened to be flanked by a wall pasted over with *dazibao*. "Quickly!" he warned, noticing the posters. "You have already attracted too much attention."

That morning I visited the house of Sun Yat-sen, who, in 1911, was elected provisional president of the newly formed Chinese republic. There I was given a badge inscribed with one of his sayings: "Everything under heaven belongs to the people." In the Peace Hotel, I had lunch with some friends. We had a clear view of the Bund, its vortex of moving protesters drawing everything and everyone into itself.

On my return to Hefei, Cao Meihua greeted me with flowers. She had taken shelter in my apartment during my absence. We went for dumplings at a local stand and caught up on the news. The class strike was still on, and a new plea had gone out from the students to the teachers. On the school bulletin board, they had pasted a fresh *dazibao*, which read:

Dear Teachers,

We have not seen each other for days. We miss you very much. This great patriotic and democratic "turmoil" has been growing up till now, but its result is still unknown. There are various indications that one bad omen has enveloped every man of insight. All kinds of expectations and suppositions have emerged here and there. Nowadays, the most conspicuous fact reveals itself to us: we, your students, already feel that our ability is falling short of our wishes. Recently, our processions and influence have become weaker and weaker, day after day. When you, our dear teachers, witness this scene, what will you feel about it—hopeful, perplexed, upset? However, at this moment, we need your support and help, for we are too exhausted to utter a single word.

Several of us tend to withdraw; some cannot even apply themselves to studying. In reality, our desire for knowledge is greater than ever. But now we are not able to settle down to read and write, because of the troops in Tiananmen Square.

Our dear teachers, come on! Please join and strengthen our ranks, both for the sake of our common fate and for the benefit of the nation!

signed,
your sincere students who are
broken-hearted and terribly scared

On the way back to the guest-house, I met Mr. Wong, a fellow teacher. "How are you?" I asked him.

"Oh, I'm fine, but the spring, China's spring, has been too short," he said wistfully.

By the middle of the week, the students were celebrating as a revolutionary martyr a first-year history student who had died in a train accident on the way home from Beijing. His classmates kept a twenty-four-hour vigil outside the dormitory where he had lived. His was a tragic loss of life. Feelings ran high. A foreign teacher took a picture of the memorial service. Someone called him a "foreign spy." That night, Cao Meihua and I sat in the *ba-jiao* grove in the dark, consulting for hours. When the time came, we wondered, how would I get out of China?

On June 1, Children's Day celebrations went forward as usual. Young pioneers, with rouge on their cheeks and red scarves tied around their necks, marched forward in groups of thirty and forty in the packed school auditorium to pledge their allegiance to the red flag of China. By June 3, I was ready for a weekend away. The tension in the city was suffocating and the humidity stifling. I boarded Bus 33 for San Chang, a ceramic tile factory my Dutch friends were setting up just outside the city. The woman sitting in front of me carried a broad basket filled with small chicks.

She spoke to me in Hefei dialect, explaining that she had paid only fifty *fen* (Chinese cents) for each chick.

Most people riding the bus were peasants returning from a day of selling produce on the free market. They knew little about the world outside, but when I asked them in Chinese if they could tell me where a very tall foreigner lived, they nodded their heads. I should get off at the last stop, they said. There, Anna and Abel waited for me. We ate Dutch pancakes for dinner. Afterwards, we walked through the fields to a neighbouring village. Seemingly unaffected by politics, the peasants used the last of the day-light hours to irrigate their paddies and plant rice. I watched one farmer steer a water buffalo as it pulled a wooden plough through the stubborn earth. His planting song filled the night with the warmth of a human presence.

The weekend passed uneventfully, with Abel and me tramping in the half-light of sun-showers through the muddy fields in knee-high boots to visit a Buddhist family and share with them a meal of tea and boiled duck eggs. On Saturday night, as we made our way to the community hall to watch the peasants play mah-jong, a monsoon descended on the village. Forbidden by the Party to gamble, the play-ers pinned clothespegs to their ears each time they lost a point. In the countryside, the night turned black and heavy with torrents of rain. We came home to listen to the VOA on the shortwave radio, but could not get a clear reception.

June 4 seemed a blessed day. In the aftermath of the storm, the countryside lay still, fresh, and quiet. The fog had lifted and we could see for miles. Hills appeared that we had not known existed, and the familiar lines of Dashu Shan punctuated the horizon. The fields of newly planted rice shimmered, a vibrant green. We decided to take a day's rest from the news; listening to the radio had become an hourly obsession. Inside his unfinished factory, Abel found a lump of leftover clay. He decided to make me a pot. He fired it in the kiln and set it on the ground to cool.

That night the jeep delivered me back to the campus.

A crowd thronged the public bulletin board. Along the main road, people huddled in small groups talking. What could have happened, I wondered. At home, I prepared a bath. I was about to step in when two students knocked on my door. "Could you come back later?" I called out.

"I think you had better let us in," they insisted.

In halting speech, they told me the story. In their own mythological terms, they described the martyrdom of young pacifists who, as they understood it, had offered themselves up in Ghandi-like waves of peaceful resistance to the troops at Tiananmen Square. Apparently, in a final bid to clear the square and crush the student movement, the People's Liberation Army had moved into the square. Some sources claimed that as many as a thousand lives had been lost. Together we wept. That night I tossed restlessly, and when I finally did drift off to sleep, I had a dream, the equivalent in my repertoire of horrors to the social tragedy of China: that a young girl had been assaulted and murdered.

The next day Wu Hong and I cycled downtown to buy a suitcase. On every corner, the VOA broadcast the news. Posters depicting the casualties in gruesome detail covered every wall in the city centre. At the main intersection, San Xiao Kou, one poster in particular commanded attention. On it, the words "China's Shame!" painted in black stood out against a background of tank tracks and bloodstains. Some students took over the traffic booths, where they wept openly. Elderly people gathered around them with a deep sadness in their faces. Other students marched around the traffic circle in the city centre, boldly making peace signs. The intersection was strewn with funeral wreaths. Above, on the overpass, hung a new slogan: "Never submit!" Some said that ambulances and troops were standing by in case anything developed. At the university, students commandeered the campus radio station and alternated funeral dirges with China's song for International Peace Year, "Let the World Be Filled with Love!" It was no time to be a spectator of demonstrations.

61

In the days immediately following June 4, shock and anger deepened into grief. Colleagues wandered the campus with swollen eyes. Disconsolate, Mr. Wong, the same teacher who had lamented the shortness of China's spring, burst spontaneously into tears when we met. "This is a tragedy, a great setback," he lamented, "a repetition of history. We are tired, so tired. We cannot bear it any longer. We have been plunged into darkness."

In the streets, an eerie silence prevailed. One by one, my students rushed for the safety of home. Only the teachers stayed on the campus. Most painful of all my students' goodbyes, Cao Meihua's parting words haunted me: "I have been changed by this change. I know I'm young, and I have much time, but . . ." She broke off as the tears glistened in her eyes and she began to weep.

"Now is the time to be strong!" I admonished her.

On June 9, Wu Li came to my rooms to say goodbye. She had been working one full year to get an exit visa and had only recently succeeded. She planned to join her husband, who was studying for a Ph.D. in the United States. She hadn't slept for days; she was terrified that the door would close and she would be separated from her husband for years. "I couldn't endure it," she cried hysterically. "I'd kill myself!"

The next day she fled the city for her home town to say goodbye to her parents. The last I heard she had boarded a riverboat for Shanghai. She took no luggage, only her two-year-old son and a purse filled with money and identification. If public transportation remained at a halt in Shanghai, she planned to walk from the waterfront all the way to the airport.

The evacuation call went out on the VOA. The Canadian Embassy urged us to leave. I could catch a charter flight from Nanjing if I could be packed in an hour, but my passport was sitting in the Foreign Affairs Office. Another charter plane was scheduled to leave from Wuhan, but I couldn't make that either. I decided to bide my time in Hefei until I could catch a direct flight to Hong Kong. The city sank into a deep, unnatural peace. Only a history teacher named Cloud—"General Cloud," I called her—dared to visit me. Deeply involved in the unfolding events, Cloud debated all night with her friends the likelihood of civil war. "It's impossible," Cloud confidently declared, and she listed the reasons.

Though she herself was tired and worn, Cloud gave me strength. She listened to me cry after I watched the full fifty minutes of government propaganda showing dead and mutilated soldiers. My heart could not distinguish between the dead of the two sides. In my mind, all were victims. Cloud oversaw the packing of my chest, disciplined me when I refused to throw out old clippings from the *China Daily*, helped me to calculate my telephone bill to the Canadian Embassy, and even protected me from a drunken suitor who found his way into my rooms late one night.

Cloud liked to grow plants, keep animals, nurture things. Most recently, she had adopted a small rabbit. She brought it with her in her purse whenever she came to visit. It was born during the first days of the student demonstrations. We called the rabbit Heping—in English, "Peace."

Two days before my June 16 departure, it rained non-stop. A deluge, a cleansing deluge rained down from the heavens onto China. "Now is the time for the healing of the wound," Hu Xiaomei remarked.

The rain made music on the broad leaves of the *ba-jiao* trees outside my window. Cloud liked to sit for hours on the balcony just listening. "The rain is too soft to make beautiful music," she would say critically, or "Now it's too hard." But sometimes she would just daydream contentedly, savouring the dense, green daylight or the darkness. At one of those times, she recalled an ancient Chinese poem:

Rain is falling on the ba-jiao leaves.
But who is there to hear it?

The last time I saw Cloud, the rain had stopped and the moon was breaking through the murky sky. Her rabbit slept peacefully in the cloth purse tied to the handlebars of her bicycle, and a stack of *China Dailies,* a parting gift from me, bulged on her rear bicycle rack. "Now no tears," she commanded. "Goodbye!"

I must have been the last Canadian to leave the country. When I phoned the embassy to say I was leaving, the attaché responded with astonishment: "Are you still here?" Even the ambassador had left the country—recalled, I was told, for consultation in Canada. I was praying that Canada wouldn't break relations with China while I was still in the country.

The airport buzzed with the anxious voices of the last foreigners scurrying to buy tickets for flights out of the country. I noticed in the crowd a well-dressed Taiwanese businessman who appeared to be cutting short a reunion, probably long awaited, with his extended family, obviously poor relations. About thirty or forty people had come to see him off. A shoulder-high barricade made of thick iron bars separated the businessman from his mainland relatives. They held out their hands. He went down the line shaking each one. The women burst into tears. As he disappeared into the departure lounge, they leaned, then almost crawled, over the fence.

The final passenger to board the plane, I turned and took one last look around me. Miles of green fields. A few men on bicycles. The countryside seemed wrapped in a deep sleep. I looked to the left. There they gathered again, the members of the family, perched on another fence. Their arms reached out, hands waving in desperate farewell, their blue cotton Mao jackets blowing in the wind. Then the plane quickly ascended, and China disappeared behind thick, grey masses of clouds.

The Shattering of the Idols, 1990

"MAKE SHANGHAI TRAIN Station a Window onto Socialist Civilization!" reads the new sign. As I wait to board the train, a military march plays and a voice booms over the loudspeaker, reciting the story of Lei Feng, the sacrificial soldier who has made a comeback in Political Study classes across the nation this past year. I am on my way to visit friends and colleagues at Anhui University, where I taught the tragedies of Shakespeare during the brief blossoming of the China spring. I haven't seen them since I left China soon after June 4. I have had a few letters, but nothing much was said, "only things have returned to normal." I wonder if it is true.

When I arrive in Hefei eight hours later, it is the peak of the afternoon and ninety degrees. Farmers squat on the street selling vegetables. Shoppers hustle home on bicycles through traffic jams. As we drive along, I notice a few changes in the scenery: a sparkling new Bank of China, a new customs house, a furniture factory, and a hotel whose name translates as "Heaven on Earth." We stop at the

Luyang Hotel, a posh hotel built only a few years ago. Already it is showing signs of age. The carpet takes on a dingy hue from repeated moppings. In places, the paint cracks and begins to peel. No foreigners sit in the lounge drinking beer, only Chinese.

Tonight I will dine in the countryside, at San Chang, with Abel. Abel resumed work on his ceramic tile factory only three weeks ago, after a long hiatus caused by economic sanctions imposed by the European Community on China one year ago. July nights in the countryside are cooler than in the city, but still hot enough to breed malarial mosquitoes. After dinner, we take our daily dose of chloroquine.

At the end of the evening, the jeep takes me back to the university. The campus is deserted. Those teachers who do remain for the summer months are sitting outdoors enjoying a feeble breeze. In the living room of Professor Wang, a fan circulates and re-circulates hot air. A whole watermelon is laid out in slices on the table. Visitors come and go, bringing me greetings, news, and small presents. The lights are off. It is too hot for lights. We sit in the dark exchanging remarks, our conversation punctuated by the waving of hand-held bamboo fans.

Madame Liu, my former Chinese teacher, is busy talking with "Teacher's Wife"—an old-fashioned term of respect, she explains to me, for Professor Wang's spouse. Professor Wang says he is feeling young for his seventy-five years. He hands me a box of chocolates, each one within shaped like an egg wrapped in brightly coloured tin foil. As he peels the wrapper from one, he wonders at how the world has changed since we last saw each other in June 1989. "Beyond my wildest dreams," he says. He speaks of "an irresistible tendency."

Professor Wang falls silent. The whirring of the fan takes over. Another two visitors, fellow teachers, drop by, having heard through the community grapevine that I am here. The professor offers them chocolates, salted nuts, a tea egg. He asks, "Will you take a glass of sweet plum juice, homemade?"

"Everything has returned to normal," one of the teachers assures me as he drinks his glass of plum juice. "The foreigners are coming back. A famous Australian writer visited the campus this past year," he explains. I ask the writer's name. Nobody quite remembers. "Paul, was it?" the teacher wonders aloud. "Perhaps he was only somewhat famous," he adds. "Anyway, he was not in our teaching group." Yes, everything has returned to normal.

Kang Li, a brilliant young teacher who studied in the United States several years ago, tells me his work on the comic elements in Shakespeare's tragedies is not progressing. He is too busy teaching English majors grammar. His thesis gathers dust on the shelf. "Anyhow," he explains, "I am revising my argument." He says he doesn't believe anymore that comedy can always be found in tragedy.

We leave Professor Wang's. Madame Liu takes me on a tour of the campus by moonlight. We walk down "Broadway," a wide avenue leading to the Party headquarters—"the White House," as the students call it. We pass a balcony where you might expect to find a Juliet calling for her Romeo, a quaint anomaly in the architecture of the Foreign Languages Department. But these days, the balcony is thronged with self-taught adult students from the countryside who have come to learn English. No soliloquies from Shakespeare's plays are intoned here.

During the past year, Madame Liu tells me, only one change has taken place on the campus: the playing field has been paved over to make a space for volleyball, basketball, and dancing. Last year, she says, the students held many open-air dances in the warm weather and in the cold. In other years, there might have been one this very night, organized by students living on campus during the summer months to cram for postgraduate exams. But the new policy set down after June Fourth, Madame Liu explains, stipulates that undergraduates can continue studies in China or abroad only after several years of working. Everyone has gone home for the summer.

I check the student dormitories just in case. Though it is past the ten o'clock curfew, the gatekeeper reluctantly lets me in. "Wu Hong! Cao Meihua!"—I call out the names of my favourite students. But their rooms are dark. The names echo in the empty corridors. Even these, the brightest students, have returned home to be with their parents. Most girls are not thinking anymore about pursuing their studies, Wu Hong told me in a letter; instead, they are looking forward to early marriage. But the dreams of adolescence still linger in the hallways. My eye is drawn to a place on the cement wall where one girl has chalked "America."

This year the students had to fight for their job assignments, Madame Liu continues. They had to plead with the leaders not to send them back to the countryside. The tendency now, she explains, is to send graduates back to their home counties to serve in the lower levels of administration. The brightest ones resist, and some, like Wu Hong and Cao Meihua, win. Both were lucky to be assigned to teach here, at a large university in the capital city.

Wu Hong, I remember vividly, was one of the first to board the free trains to Beijing last spring. She did not tell her mother she had gone to camp in Tiananmen Square. Very few girls actually camped in the square, she told me on her return. This past year Wu Hong had to undergo intensive re-education, write self-criticisms, and parrot the political coach, Mr. Yu. She succeeded in convincing him that her involvement in the student movement was only a temporary lapse. Now Wu Hong believes it was a mistake to demonstrate for change. So much suffering, she confided to me in a letter, and no result. A tragedy.

At the English Corner, the local meeting place where the Chinese come to practise English with foreigners and each other, I seek out more of my students. I want to speak to them firsthand, but will they speak openly to me? Luckily, I find Mr. Chen, the former monitor in my third-year class. He has been assigned to the Foreign Trade Department and is pleased about this development.

"Have there been any changes?" I ask him after we have exchanged greetings.

"The economy has improved a little," he says cautiously, "but only so-so."

Another student, this one from the night school downtown, elaborates. A tall and sophisticated man, Mr. Sun is carrying a bar of Camay soap in his hand. He is astonished to see me, he says. I ask about recent social changes. "The socialist civilization marches forward," he answers wryly.

There is one last stop: the local church. No foreign teachers or businessmen sit in the front pews these days. They have all gone home. The missionaries from America are the only foreigners in attendance now, and even their numbers have greatly diminished. None of my students are here, but the theology students gather near the chancel. I wonder if there have been any changes for them. The church is packed, mostly with workers and peasants. Simple people, for the most part women with cropped, grey hair, crouch on tiny stools in the aisles. They listen intently and watch carefully everything that happens, occasionally wiping the perspiration from their brows with handkerchiefs.

The benediction is given. The hymn, a relic from the days of the Methodist missionaries, is sung. The pastor launches into his sermon. The text is 1 Kings 2, the story of how God punished Solomon, who was drawn to the worship of idols, by taking away most of his kingdom. The pastor elaborates on his theme, recounting how in the last days of the kings of Judah, Josiah arose and destroyed the idols in an effort to abate the anger of the God of Israel and save what was left of the kingdom of Judah. But the God of Israel would not be appeased and, in the end, the kingdom fell. Every Chinese in the congregation immediately recognizes the political moral of the sermon.

It is my last night in Hefei. I return to San Chang for a farewell dinner with Abel, now the only foreign businessman left in the city. The missionaries are here just for the summer months, to teach at the education institute. Soon they will return to America and the city will belong, once again, completely to the Chinese. At San Chang, the dusk falls softly. The coal trucks from Huainan in the north rattle along the dark highway. The chef, Mr. Qu, finishes washing the supper dishes. It is still almost ninety degrees. I get up and go to the window in search of a faint hint of a breeze. I notice the screen has been ripped off to let in more air. There is nothing between me and the outside: I look through the window of a socialist civilization.

The People's Park, 1992

NOVEMBER 12. A GOLDEN DAY in Shanghai. Deep in the heart of the People's Park, I wander and dream. When I arrive at the entrance to the park, I cannot find the small change I need to pay the admission fee. An elderly woman, dressed in the kind of plain blue pantsuit often worn by Chinese women of her generation, appears like a fairy god-mother, holding out one *yuan* (Chinese dollars). She pays the gatekeeper then smiles at me, shooing me as she does into the verdure of the inner sanctum.

My ears still ring with the complaints of the taxi driver who brought me here: the economy, politics, living conditions in Shanghai, the traffic. Complaints and their flip side, a litany of newborn hopes in China: prosperity, happiness, a future. More than a roof over one's head and an iron rice-bowl. But as I walk, the echo of the taxi driver's lamentations, like the accumulated dust of my journey, fades away.

I stroll inside the People's Park. Life unfolds all around me. A group of middle-aged women practises tai chi in a circle. A group of elderly men plays cards. A young couple walks with a child. I take up the rhythm of Chinese life, losing myself in its pattern. Why worry? At times like this, I know I am only a single thread in the tapestry.

Two lovers laugh on a park bench. They remind me of another pair of lovers I saw in Hangzhou two days earlier while visiting a Buddhist temple. The Hangzhou lovers strolled in front of me, obscured by a veil of incense smoke. As we toured the temple together, the great statues towered over us: Amitabha, Guanyin, and other, lesser deities. The smoke of burning incense overpowered us. We watched as the older pilgrims kowtowed.

The eyes of the young couple grew wide with curiosity. They were not really pilgrims, I concluded, but tourists just like me. They, too, were strangers, looking with fascination on the old gods. To me, they seemed lost, wandering through the veils of incense as through vales of illusion. Where would they find their truth?

I snap back to the present. The lovers on the park bench are leaving me, moving off and taking their own mysterious, self-enclosed world with them, a golden world made for a golden day in Shanghai. I am wandering through the park aimlessly now, killing time before I meet an older couple, she the chair of an English Department and he a publisher, whom I got to know during the spring of 1989. I am sure they want to reminisce, to call up memories of times past—the sorrow and the joy. But I am not quite ready to meet them yet. Just a little more walking in the People's Park, a little more fresh air, a little more green, then it will be time.

I continue to walk. How interesting it is, I reflect, that the Chinese so love parks. Parks and intricately planned gardens—they are everywhere in China, in every nook and cranny of even the crassest, most industrial cities. Is it a devotion to beauty? An enduring respect for the harmony of creation with roots in Taoism? As I stroll, I begin to daydream, remembering a night in Hangzhou when I walked with friends around West Lake.

That night, the weeping willows had touched the tips of their branches so gracefully to the water, as they do in Chinese paintings and ancient poems. Like so many scenes of natural beauty in China, this one was exquisite. The haunting reflection of the moonlight on the lake spurred us to philosophical musings. While we sat talking, a boy of about ten appeared mysteriously from behind the willow trees. He came up to us, attracted by the music of our speech, and just stared. We stopped talking and gazed back at him. He smiled, then ambled off into the night.

And now, on this golden day in Shanghai, this most golden day of autumn, another child, a girl this time, comes up to me and stares right into my eyes. I say hello. She doesn't answer, but follows me as I wander. I am deep in the heart of the park now. Will I be able to find my way back in time to meet my friends? If only I hadn't spent so much time in Pudong this morning. The name means "east of the Huangpu River." Pudong is the mecca of every Chinese business person in Shanghai, a great, new economic development zone connected to the city by a bridge the locals take pride in comparing to San Francisco's Golden Gate Bridge.

Now I must hurry: I am late. There is no more time for dreaming. My friends will be waiting. I must find my way out of this massive labyrinth of green. I walk only a short distance before I find myself close to a street. Luckily, it is the very street I am looking for. There are my friends. They are waving to me and smiling. I am walking hurriedly. As I come within earshot, I hear them call out in voices rich in sincerity, "Welcome back to China! It is so good to have you with us again!"

The Letter, 1994

I HAVE BECOME A WOMAN of letters. Everyone I am connected to by that intimate web of relationships we call
friendship lives on the other side of the world. How can my
roots have crept so far afield to another land? I spent my
childhood summers on my grandmother's farm, so I
believe in the power of growing things to follow their own
destiny—zinnias in long, straight rows, such as my grandmother used to grow, and sweet peas nestled in curling
wisps of vines—and so I accept.

Plants follow the light; even roots, when exposed, creep
towards it. And light often comes from unexpected
sources. So I sit on the porch these mornings under the
fickle September sun, now bright, now faint, writing letters,
endless letters to the world. I am trying to touch others
with the paper I touch. And I can only hope the right hand
responds to that gentle touch. Nothing worse than to
squeeze a hand tightly that will not respond in kind, or to
touch a hand that withdraws. So I write generously, cautiously, packaging my soul in a four-by-six-inch envelope

and casting it to the wind with all the desperate abandon of an island hostage throwing a bottle with a message in it into the wide and unforgiving sea.

Why write at all, even if it is only letters? "Writing and painting," wrote Chang Yen-yuan in the ninth century, "have different names but a common body." Or as a Song dynasty poet wrote of two eighth-century masters:

> The writings of Shao Ling are paintings
> without forms;
> The paintings of Han Kan are poems without words.

Poetry, calligraphy, painting—in ancient China, these three arts were called "the three perfections." To write a letter is to make a poem, a painting, a piece of art. At best, to inscribe the page is to create a work of art and live forever. At worst, it is to extinguish oneself finally, fiercely. As Walter Pater put it, "To burn always with this hard, gemlike flame, to maintain this ecstasy, is success in life."

With sadness and with longing, I remember especially the letter I promised Hu Xiaomei. Hu dreamed of us growing old together, she told me, of sending letters across the ocean that separated us. It was such a large ocean, one that would never shrink. We both knew we could not cross it, but we hoped our letters, a veritable spate of carefully premeditated scrawls and scratches, could. Faint etchings on an old stone, to be deciphered by scientists in future times and still not understood. Hieroglyphs on the face of eternity.

But for Hu Xiaomei, the expected letter has never arrived. For her, life will be a strange mélange of waiting moments until the final letter, the omega, is inscribed. Then it will no longer matter. Beginnings and endings. Alpha and omega. "How are you?" to the final salutation. Though she yearned to study abroad, Hu promised me she would stay in China as long as I did, and she kept her word. The year after I left China, she left too, forced to abandon her husband and daughter if she wished to pursue her dream of graduate studies at the University of California.

That was five years ago. Once she sent me a postcard from the coast. I replied with one from New York City, where I was visiting. Her postcard was tentative, exploratory. Mine was awkward, formal—unable to bridge the gap. I was glad she had gone abroad, I wrote, since I knew that was what she wanted. I was proud that she was pursuing her studies. Visit New York City, I urged, the mecca of North American culture. But I couldn't help asking, "Was it all worth it after all?"

Hu would have sighed over that final question, remembering, remembering. . . . Though she was a fellow teacher, a peer, Hu sat in on my Shakespeare class. She read the part of Romeo, and I, Juliet. At dance parties in China, it is common for people of the same sex to dance together. At such parties, Hu, a much better dancer than I, would lead me in the rumba and the waltz. One night a week, we moonlighted together, teaching English at night school downtown. On those nights I would stand just beneath her second-storey window and call out: "Hu Xiaomei! Hu Xiaomei! Where art thou, Hu Xiaomei?" The light would switch off and Hu would emerge with her bicycle, laughing.

I loaned Hu Alice Munro's novella, *Lives of Girls and Women*. There was so little stimulation on the campus and Hu was hungry for new books. She stayed up all night reading. The next day she told me the book had proven to her that women's experience is universal. Once a friend loaned her a biography of the early-twentieth-century comedienne Fanny Brice. Hu was so fascinated by her story that she translated it into Chinese. Throughout the year, Hu and I were constant companions. She made me *babaofan*, organized class outings for me, and took me boating at Xiaoyaojin Park. Despite the differences in our cultures, we thought we had understood each other perfectly.

Gradually, I saw less of Hu. Then, she did not come to visit my rooms anymore. I wondered what had happened.

No one seemed to know. One day, in Shakespeare class, Mr. Gu read from *Othello,*

> But jealous souls will not be answered so;
> They are not ever jealous for the cause,
> But jealous for they're jealous. 'Tis a monster
> Begot upon itself, born on itself.

Hu, who still sat in on my class, looked at me, and I looked at her. Suddenly I understood: the others were suspicious of her motives. They were jealous that I might help her to go abroad to study. In order to prove the sincerity of her friendship, Hu had had to end it.

I remembered a Chinese film I had seen some years ago, long before I had thought about going to China. I hadn't understood the film then. About a love relationship, not a friendship, *The Old Well* showed how tightly knit the fabric of social relationships is in China and how it can smother genuine human affection. The hero and heroine of the movie have always loved each other, but due to the complexities of politics and the social relationships in the village where they live, they have never been able to consummate their love in a marriage. Then, unexpectedly, they find themselves trapped together in an old well. There, at last, in the blessed social void created by the well, they are able to open their hearts to one another and express their love—until they are rescued. Then their charade must begin again.

I had hoped that when Hu came to America we could resume our friendship. But I learned that it is not always possible to transplant the fragile flower of friendship to a new soil. The last I heard, Hu had dropped out of the graduate program for lack of funding and was selling hamburgers in San Francisco, or was that just another rumour, more gossip? One of China's lost generation, Hu deserved more. I wept for her when I heard that, especially since I knew it had not been the fate of others to sell hamburgers.

Less than ten years younger than Hu, Wu Li had landed a job as a high-level executive with a multi-million-dollar
corporation and was living, I heard, with her husband and
child in a trendy suburb of Washington, D.C. But how
could I convey my feelings to Hu now? She had kept her
side of our pact: she had stayed in China as long as I had.
Now we were both in America, but we no longer had the
common ground upon which to continue our friendship.
A new world with new rules. The gap between us was now
wider than just an ocean.

Letters of separation. Letters of reunion. Letters with
roots and letters mirroring the stars. Letters of the living
and letters of the dead. How is it that letters enshrine what
we cannot speak? Inscribed memory. A sad genre, letters,
except business letters, the only tolerable form, standing
like mountains among the clouds—granite, steadfast,
unmovable. The hard currency of human interchange.

Letters. What good are they anyway? Suddenly I imagine the great pile of letters I have written to and received
from China swirling in the eye of a tornado, a flock of
letters taking flight into the heavens, a whirling cone to
scatter words, like a pack of cards falling where it may. The
dice, the final throw in this great game of connection, to be
tallied on the Judgement Day. On that day, I shall finish the
letter I am composing in my mind, my omega, in which I
request Hu Xiaomei's forgiveness for my failure to write.

I have lost touch with many of my Chinese friends and
students now that they have come to North America. For
them, life is faster; there is no time to talk or write. They
are busy making money, getting degrees, making life better—for the future. But still I wait for a letter postmarked
"China," a letter containing words of comfort, perhaps
even a revelation. I am waiting to hear if the sun still rises
over the Lake of Tears in a glory of pink rays and if the
King of Heaven and his seven daughters still shine down
on the balcony of Room 202 of the Foreign Guest-house at
night. I'd like to know if Old Liu still sits, sphinx-like, in

front of the gatehouse, and if the old people still practise tai chi on the shores of the Lake of Tears at dawn. I'd like to know if the rain still falls on my *ba-jiao* grove, and if there is anyone left to hear it.

DREAMS

Dreams, broken or intact—there was no one I met in China who did not have them. Not secret ambitions people harbour of achieving greatness or renown, but dreams of the heart, quintessentially personal dreams reflecting the quest of the yearning soul in search of what will bring it light and glory.

I found such dreams everywhere, not only in student dormitories where they might be expected to flourish, but in the eyes of peasant children and middle-aged workers. As I learned, no system of politics, no matter how much it advocates the sacrifice of the individual for the common good, can extinguish the desire for happiness and fulfilment in its most uniquely personal forms.

For many, the dream took the form of a yearning to go abroad. But that yearning, I became convinced, was just a symbol of the need for a wider, more spacious country of the heart in which to roam and dwell. The minds and souls of my Chinese friends hungered after a new land where they could become more truly themselves.

They longed to see themselves as figures on a new ground, and expressed that longing in myriad ways: in a fascination with a tall, blonde foreigner, a symbol of complete "otherness," of impossible things that might become possible; or in an obsession with pursuing studies in the West. For Ding Liang, the longing took shape as an irrepressible urge to do what Huck Finn had done: "light out for the Territory ahead of the rest" in search of that phantasm—personal freedom. And for Klee Wyck, it manifested itself in anxiety rooted in the fear "What is going to happen to me?"

But in all my Chinese friends, the impulse to fulfil their dreams ebbed and flowed like the waves, in response to the shifting social and political forces. At some times, it seemed more plausible to harbour dreams than at others. Some think that June 4, 1989, marked the death of dreams, but perhaps, after all, it signalled the beginning of a new era in China, a time of reflection and searching.

Dreams—some broken, some still in their earliest flowering, and some yet unborn, all revealing worlds of heartfelt longing and secret fire. I was continually amazed at the capacity of my Chinese friends to live in possibility when there seemed to be no hope of translating possibilities into realities. Was it an innate hopefulness, or a refusal to surrender? Over time, some did realize their dreams. Others did not, but continued to dream nevertheless. These ones I will always remember.

A Canadian Cheese Comes to Hefei

THE CHINESE HESITATE TO SAY it, but to them cheese is the foulest importation of Western culture ever to infiltrate China. It is even more threatening to the Chinese well-being than eating sandwiches for lunch instead of rice and a hot vegetable dish, and, certainly, it leaves as bad a taste in your mouth.

But in my country cheese is a local hero, especially cheddar cheese. Canada is famous for it, and any Canadian worthy of the name will long for a slice or two every now and then wherever he or she is living in the world. Cheddar cheese is part of the national identity, a much-needed symbol of solidarity in a mosaic of diverse cultures always threatening to break back down into fragments of glass.

That wasn't why my mother decided to send me a cheddar cheese a few weeks after I left for China in early September. She sent it as an emissary of love and as a reminder of home, but also as a test—of the cheese, of myself, of the nation as a whole. Could the cheese survive the journey? Could it penetrate the Bamboo Curtain?

Could it retain its identity so far abroad? Would it taste the same in the far reaches of mainland China?

The cheese set out in a ten-by-ten brown box with a bag of jujubes, a Milky Way and a Snickers bar, a Penguin history of Canada, a book by Northrop Frye on Shakespeare for my graduate course on his plays, and a set of thermal long underwear for the winter. The cheese had already breezed its way through the shipping bureaucracy on the Canadian side, my mother wrote me. I imagined it setting sail on a slow boat to China.

Several weeks later I received a letter from the customs office in Nanjing. Actually, the letter wasn't addressed to me, and even if it had been I couldn't have read it, since it was written in Chinese characters. Mr. Qing, the head of the *Waiban* (Foreign Affairs Office), brought me the letter, explaining that the box had arrived, but it would take time to clear customs. "Xiao deng yihui'er" (Wait a little), he said. The cheese, I also found out from Mr. Qing, had not come on a slow boat to China; it had been flown in by Air China weeks ago and had been sitting all that time in Nanjing.

The cheese had travelled thousands of miles, from Toronto to Nanjing. The rest of the journey, from Nanjing to Hefei, was only a four-hour train ride. I imagined slicing off a piece of my cheese and placing it on top of the gooey white bread for sale at the campus store. I brewed myself a cup of Chinese tea in my lidded white-and-blue dragon mug, then sat back in a chair in my rooms at the guesthouse. Wu Li drank with me, but she didn't share my confidence at all. Anyway, she wasn't looking forward to her first sliver of Canadian cheese, though she had politely agreed to try it. I knew she was in this with me purely for the sake of friendship.

Wu Li and her son, Xiao Bo Bo, lived in the teachers' dormitory next to mine. Wu Li's husband had gone to study for a Ph.D. at the University of Michigan. When Wu Li was not wading through red tape to get a visa to join her husband, she was helping me. She was my "coordinator," assigned by the dean of the Foreign Languages Department to look after me. Her job was to cater to all the whims, wants, and needs of the foreigner—in the mind of any Chinese a virtually impossible task.

You had to be versatile and ingenious to survive such an assignment. Being a dutiful person, she took the job seriously, but duty soon turned to friendship as she and I discovered a common love of modern poetry. I think Wu Li was the only colleague I had on campus who truly enjoyed Ezra Pound's *Cantos* and who thrilled at the opening lines of T. S. Eliot's *The Waste Land*: "April is the cruelest month. . . ." In Hefei, April is the most lyrical of spring months, with blossoms of all kinds, especially peach and apple, adorning the orchards near Dashu Shan, the local mountains. Still, Eliot's lines struck some chord in Wu Li's being, and she understood and responded.

When Wu Li came to my room one golden autumn day to sip tea and talk about Pound and Eliot, I raised the subject of the cheese. Had it or had it not passed through customs? How would it get from Nanjing to Hefei? And most pressing, what condition would the cheese be in when it arrived? Wu Li was dreading more and more her first bite of Canadian cheese. But since in China it is a duty to honour your parents, to Wu Li it would have seemed disrespectful to refuse to taste my mother's cheese. She began to steel herself for the battle: it would be her nose versus the cheese, with myself as the only referee.

Two weeks after I received the letter from Nanjing, Mr. Qing told us the cheese had passed through customs at last. Wu Li and I celebrated with hot powdered milk and peanut brittle. Soon my mother's cheese would be sitting on my table. How would I keep the cheese once it arrived, I wondered. Was there a refrigerator somewhere in the guest-house? The next afternoon, as I was preparing my lectures, Ye Ye called to me in Chinese: "Come down and see! A box has arrived for you!" I ran down the stairs.

In the guest-house foyer sat a box framed by five happy faces: Lao Zheng, Ye Ye, Zhong Mei, Chen, and Mr. Tan. They all stood around, grinning and looking at me to gauge my response. It was one of the largest boxes I had ever seen. In fact, it was not a box at all but a refrigerator, one of the most coveted possessions of all newly married couples in China. It was a green refrigerator covered with cardboard, a green refrigerator disguised as a box.

The three men who had brought the refrigerator carried it upstairs and ripped the cardboard off. I plugged it in. Everyone stood around silently, watching it grow cold by degrees. I was puzzled. I hadn't asked for a refrigerator. I had no kitchen to cook in, so why would I buy anything that needed refrigeration? Except for the cheese and a few stray bottles of "sour milk," as the homemade yoghurt we bought on campus was called, I had nothing to fill its empty shelves. Still, the arrival of the fridge seemed to signal that some cosmic force was on our side, so I said in Chinese "Kuaile!" (Happy!), but it came out "Huaile!" (Broken!), and it took some time to remove the looks of consternation from the faces of those who thought of themselves as my deliverers.

The fridge stood empty in the middle of my living-room. The golden days of October grew shorter and shorter. Wu Li and I began to huddle under blankets and keep our coats on when we drank tea in my room. We spoke of many things: the poetry of Shelley, the sonnets of Shakespeare, the novels of Thomas Hardy, and, of course, the cheese. We wondered how the cheese, having passed through customs weeks ago, had gotten stuck in Nanjing. Wu Li suggested we ask one of the university's drivers to pick up the cheese for us. So what if it cost a small fee? It would be worth it.

Mr. Lu drove a sleek, grey European-made car. He was in his early forties, a short and wiry man with all the bravado of a stock-car racer, probably from his long experience driving on Chinese roads. Mr. Lu wore black imitation-leather gloves whenever he drove. When he wasn't driving, you could find him strutting around his car, lending a final touch to its polish. Mr. Lu was not the least bit interested in bringing the cheese to Hefei.

Wu Li tried to get to know Mr. Lu better. She visited his home several times and took gifts of Chinese tea and cigarettes, items Mr. Lu would appreciate. He seemed pleased, lifting the right side of his lip in a slight smile. After a while, Wu Li gave up on visiting Mr. Lu.

About this time, my mother called me long distance. It was one of the few times she managed to get through the Chinese operators and the guest-house staff, most of whom spoke no English. They were like a series of walls to scale, but my mother was determined and she passed over them all. In a letter, I had told her to say "Ha Qisen" and spelled it out for her phonetically. She had said it, over and over again, and she had succeeded. She wanted to know how I was and how did I like the cheese?

The cheese was becoming an obsession. That evening, as I tried to run myself a hot bath and got only cold water, my thoughts circled back to it. How could I allow my mother's cheese, so carefully wrapped, to sit in a customs house in Nanjing for all these weeks? Why hadn't I taken action? Didn't I care?

As these thoughts were running like cold water through my mind, Wu Li knocked at my door. I called to her to come in. She found me in the bathroom, sitting on the edge of the tub in my People's Liberation Army coat with tears running down my cheeks. "What's wrong?" she asked.

"My mother's cheese!" I blurted out over the crash of the cold, running water.

Wu Li had had enough. Really enough. Everything in China was so slow and backward, she exclaimed. "Look at me, trying to get my visa for one full year and spending every minute I'm not with you on it!" The cheese was becoming a symbol of all our griefs and frustrations, our dreams and our hopes. If only we could get the cheese, all would be well. We just knew it.

Wu Li stormed out of the room. I turned off the cold bath water and ran after her. Was there something I hadn't thought of, some last, desperate plan Wu Li had kept from me? She was walking past the gatehouse, past Old Liu who, despite the cold November winds, slept in his chair, down the dirt road towards the east gate of the campus. I followed closely, calling out after her. She turned down the path of the Professors' Building, walked in the door, and climbed three flights of stairs. We stood in front of a closed door. Wu Li knocked. I waited to see what would happen next.

The president of the university, Professor Du, opened the door. He was a calm, sophisticated man in his late fifties, an electronics engineer who had studied in the United States and often travelled abroad. Without a single word of introduction, Wu Li pointed at me and wailed, "She wants her mother's cheese!" Professor Du showed no sign of surprise; he simply invited us in and asked his wife to bring us two cups of warm milk sweetened with sugar. We settled into the couch and Wu Li, almost in tears, told the tale of the wanderings of the Canadian cheese.

When she had finished, President Du looked very gravely at us, from one to the other. "I think it will be possible to bring the cheese to Hefei by tomorrow," he said. After we had sipped the last of our hot milk, we excused ourselves. Before we left, the president told me how pleased he was to meet me. In fact, he said, he had a daughter who was going to Canada. Perhaps I could meet her sometime? She wanted to start an import-export business. Would I know anything about that? I agreed to do all I could to help with the business. As Wu Li and I walked down the stairs we felt as light as the falling leaves whirling all around us. The cheese would be coming to Hefei by tomorrow. Wu Li acted as if she could hardly wait.

At about three o'clock the next day, Mr. Lu came to my door with a ten-by-ten box. Wu Li and I had just come from teaching classes at the Foreign Languages Department. We huddled in my rooms, wearing black cotton gloves to keep our hands warm as we sipped our tea. Stone-faced, Mr. Lu handed over the box. We thanked him profusely. He said nothing as he backed out the door.

Wu Li and I placed the box in the middle of the floor and stared for a minute in disbelief: it was really here! I ripped the string off the box and opened it. Nestled between the book on Shakespeare, the Penguin history of Canada, and the package of jujubes, the cheese lay wrapped in tin foil, thermal underwear, and brown paper bags. I removed the tin foil at last. Except for the outer layer, the cheese had weathered the journey well. I remembered my mother's stories of my grandfather's cheese in the days before the refrigerator. He had simply scraped off the moulding exterior to reveal the creamy orange surface underneath. I did the same.

Wu Li sat and watched. I knifed off a sliver of cheese for myself and tasted it with relish. I asked Wu Li if she would like to sample it, assuring her that I wouldn't be offended if she didn't. She insisted on trying it. I knew she was saying it just to please me, but I also knew how important it was for her to save face by keeping her promise. So I sliced her a piece and turned away as she ate. After she had finished, I glanced in her direction. Her face had a look of genuine pleasure on it. "It's delicious!" Wu Li exclaimed.

She encouraged me to eat more, while she leafed through the books. By the time we had finished unpacking, Wu Li had to pick up Xiao Bo Bo from the nursery. Before she left, we placed the Canadian cheese ceremoniously in the refrigerator. I walked, as is the custom in China, downstairs to the guest-house door to see Wu Li off and thanked her for all her help in retrieving the cheese.

I went back upstairs to straighten up the room, which was littered with papers, books, and the other contents of the box. At last, there was only one item left to be discarded: the white serviette I had used to pass Wu Li her slice of

Canadian cheese. I picked it up, ready to crumple it and toss it into the waste basket. But the serviette was bulkier than it should have been for a mere piece of paper. I could feel something hidden inside it. I unfolded it. There was Wu Li's slice of cheese, with the tiniest peck, a peck such as a bird would make, of a nibble on its upper edge.

As I said at the beginning, to the Chinese, cheese is the foulest importation of Western culture. Though the taste may be all right, cheese has a scent intolerable to the nostrils. Looking at it from the other side, I have to admit that I have slipped many finely roasted chicken feet under my plate. It takes time to cultivate the taste buds for such delicacies of Chinese cuisine when you have been raised on bread and porridge and tea.

Some time ago, Wu Li wrote me from Michigan. There was something she wanted to confess: she had never eaten my mother's cheese that day and regretted her disrespect to my parent. But since there is some cosmic force of justice in the world—Wu Li called it fate—she had received her punishment on the day she started her classes at the University of Michigan. The dean had invited the new students to a wine and cheese party at the Faculty Club. Wu Li ended up sitting right next to the dean. He offered her a piece of cheese. To refuse would be unthinkable, so she looked for the familiar orange kind, then muttered the brief incantation "Her mother's cheese!" and ate her fill.

Klee Wyck

I was working on a big totem with heavy woods behind. How badly I want that nameless thing! First there must be an idea, a feeling, or whatever you want to call it, the something that interested or inspired you sufficiently to make you desire to express it. . . . Then you must discover the pervading direction, the pervading rhythm, the dominant, recurring forms. . . .
——*Emily Carr, "Hundreds and Thousands"*

KLEE WYCK WAS MAO HUA'S Haida name. I gave it to her one afternoon when some of the teachers gathered at Fuyang Teachers' College for tea with me, the visiting foreign expert. Foreigners who live in China usually acquire at least one Chinese name. I myself have collected four over the years: Hu Jinle, or "Happy Silk"; Hu Shanhua, or "Mountain of Prosperity"; Xu Yazhu, or "Graceful Bamboo"; and Ha Qisen, or "Laughing in a Beautiful Jade Forest."

Mao Hua had never had an English name; neither had her colleagues. From their excitement at the prospect, I got the impression that having an English name was a bit like hiking through a valley and sighting suddenly, through clouds of mist, a distant mountain. It gave you a surprise and an unexpected view.

I went around the room. Next to me sat Florence, the self-sacrificing teacher who went to her students' bedsides when they were ill, a modern-day Florence Nightingale without the candle. Beside Florence mused Jane, a romantic woman of passionate sensibility who echoed in her being the wild, untamed spirit of Jane Eyre. Opposite me in the circle stared Marie, the coolly dispassionate scientist who carried forward in her research the spirit of her namesake, Marie Curie. Beside her smiled Serena, a calm and expansive soul who had found her happiness roaming the remote deserts of Xinjiang in the northwest of China.

Last in the circle sat Klee Wyck—"Laughing One." It was what the Haida people called Emily Carr, the renowned Canadian painter who had studied the late impressionist style in Paris before returning to the west coast of Canada to capture the spirit world of the Indian peoples in oils. The name suited Mao Hua for the same reasons it suited Emily Carr: she was never afraid, never arrogant, and she knew how to laugh.

In most ways, Mao Hua was like any other teacher at the university. Of average height, she had a great head of bluntly cut black hair that hung thickly at her shoulders. From behind that black mass, her eyes peered out at you through dark-rimmed glasses set against the background of a remarkably round face. Mao dressed simply in tight black pants and a short pink jacket that flared out, 1950s style, at the bottom.

But in one respect, Mao Hua distinguished herself from her peers. When she smiled, her typically Chinese demure was shattered by an immodestly wide Cheshire-cat grin revealing almost all of her pearly white teeth. And when she laughed, Mao changed from a shy, inhibited young woman into a wild and spirited creature that gave you the feeling it could never be caught or tamed.

When Mao Hua first heard her Indian name, she stared out at me from under the heavy fringe of bangs that fell along the top of her glasses, surprised, cautious, tentative. But when I explained the name, I could see that she liked its meaning and was pleased to be distinguished from the other teachers by an Indian name.

As the dean's liaison, Mao Hua was the guardian of an elaborate program set up for me by the college. At lectures, meetings, and banquets, she had to deal with everyone from university officials and the hotel manager to the dining-room chef and the university driver, who preferred to keep his own schedule. Her job was to monitor everything I saw and heard and probably to report everything I said.

Although Mao didn't stay in my room with me, she did stay in the hotel, in a cramped room with two narrow cots, one for her and one for the hotel maid. We ate every meal together. We took walks in the Chinese garden at the hotel, or in the parking lot just inside the Ming dynasty-style gates, but I noticed that Mao Hua never suggested we walk outside the gates of the "luxury" hotel itself.

I think the officials in charge of my visit were afraid some sign of backwardness or poverty would mar the image they thought they had so successfully conveyed of Fuyang as a thriving, modern city of the New China, what the colourful tourist brochure given me on my arrival described as the "bridge of Shanghai Economically Co-ordinated Region to the Northwest part of China" and "the pivot of communication in the Northwest." But it was not possible to hide the secret of Fuyang: the town was as desolate and lonely as Emily Carr's Skedans or Tanoo, and almost as isolated. At its heart rang a great loneliness, and you felt that the Tourist Bureau would do better to weave legends from this than to spend energy hiding it.

Throughout my weeklong stay, Mao Hua and I were bound together in the skein of my schedule. Moving with me in my curious foreigner's world, she had many new experiences. Mao had never ridden in a car before and she couldn't open the door, so, giggling wildly, she ran around to my door and slipped in beside me. She laughed as I struggled to eat with chopsticks the "Western" breakfast touted by the hotel menu: a single rubbery egg lying in a pool of water and a piece of bread that looked as if it had been toasted over a campfire.

During the day, Mao Hua rushed me about frenetically, Chinese style, from activity to activity. Once, as she ran ten steps ahead of me in the street, I called out in exasperation, "What's the rush?"

"China is a developing country," she called back over her shoulder. "We must catch up."

"But even China can take an afternoon off, can't it?" I shouted back.

"Is it true?" she replied in her own characteristically unidiomatic English.

One afternoon, when we had a few spare minutes, Mao Hua took me to her dormitory to show me the room she shared with another young teacher, also single and in her twenties. It was a Spartan room—cement walls and cement floors—but maintained with care. A small, homey-looking rug lay in the middle of the cold floor beside the bed. A few pictures covered the walls, scenes of distant and exotic places that Mao Hua, assigned to Fuyang Teachers' College for life, could never hope to visit.

At dinner time, Mao drilled me on the Chinese words she had taught me that day. In my notebooks from that time, I find various phrases written in her own hand in pinyin—for example, "Zaoshang hao, tongxuemen!" (Good morning, classmates!), or "Duibuqi, cesuo huaile" (There is something wrong with the toilet).

But at night we would take things "Indian time," with Klee Wyck stories and jokes on the trickster gods who ruled our lives: the hotel chef; my faltering toilet; the maid who served, or rather mostly failed to serve, my room; and the Party secretary who was taking my visit so seriously.

During the quiet evening hours we shared at the hotel, Mao Hua never spoke of herself. After we had finished my Chinese lesson for the day, she wanted to hear more about Klee Wyck. I tried to describe what totem poles looked like, with their sharp-beaked ravens and squatting bears; to tell her what they signified to the Indians; and to explain why Emily Carr had been so interested in sketching and painting them.

I told her how earthly creatures like the raven and supernatural beings like Qaganjaat spoke to the tribe, telling it stories about the creation of the world and how to live in it. I introduced her to the Indians' trickster gods who, like the Monkey King of Chinese legend, enjoyed playing pranks on unsuspecting humans.

But Mao Hua liked the stories of my own travels through Klee Wyck country best: the glory of sailing up the Inside Passage at dawn, past cannery towns and isolated Native settlements, with the dark shadows of forests looming up on either side of the boat. I told her about my visit to Massett on the northern island of the Queen Charlottes, where some sun-drenched poles still kept vigil, facing towards the bay, as if ready to greet a visitor arriving by canoe.

I told Mao about camping for ten days in the rain on the beach near Massett, how each afternoon, when the tide was out, we harvested Alaskan king crabs, cooked them in a rain-drenched fire, then dispersed the butter-soaked remains and empty shells far down the beach to protect our campsite from marauding bears.

Mao Hua never got enough of these Klee Wyck stories. By the end of the week, she began to tell the stories back to me, with her own embellishments, and to make up her own stories about what Klee Wyck might do in various situations.

One night I tried to describe to Mao Hua one of my favourite Emily Carr paintings, *Scorned as Timber, Beloved of the Sky*. The theme of the painting was simple: a single tree, bathed in an oblique and mysterious light, stood apart from its fellows, deep in the heart of a dense rain forest. But it was difficult to describe in words exactly what the images conveyed. In the painting, a very tall, ethereal, majestic pine seemed to be stretching its branches heavenward, as if yearning to commune with something beyond itself, or seeking some place in a greater pattern. It was often like this in Emily Carr's paintings, I told Mao Hua. "Each thing is connected somehow to every other thing."

She replied, "You know, in Chinese we say, 'The wind always knocks down the tree that stands higher than the rest. The people's words will destroy someone who stands out from the mass.' "

Mao Hua paused and then said, "I wonder if Klee Wyck ever felt sad in those places with only totems to talk to."

"Sometimes she must have felt lonely," I said, "but probably not so lonely as someone else might feel, since she had learned the language of the totems and could hear their stories. Other times, when she was sleeping, the totem poles frightened her with their noisy talk. But often the very loneliness of a village made her long to return to it," I told Mao, recalling some stories from Carr's own published journals.

On my last night in Fuyang, Mao Hua grew quiet and withdrawn. She didn't want to hear my Klee Wyck stories, or tell any of her own.

"What's wrong?" I asked.

"It's hard to explain."

"But you look so sad."

"Yes, it's sadness. All the students and young teachers at the college have it."

"But what is it?"

"It's hard to explain."

"Hu Shanhua," she said the next morning as we walked in the hotel parking lot, "may I suggest to you that we walk to the Wenfeng Tower?"

The Wenfeng Tower dominated the skyscape of Fuyang like a totem from a past civilization. In English it was called the Tower of Questions. It had been built after one of the great battles of the famous General Cao Cao, who had once lived in the region, to encourage a people great in military might to cultivate the life of the mind. I wondered if the tower still spoke to the people of Fuyang, or if it had become silent, like the abandoned totems in Emily Carr's paintings. I wanted to know whether there was anyone left who could understand its questions or who cared enough to try.

"Yes, of course, I would like to visit the Wenfeng Tower," I answered, curious to know why Klee Wyck had suddenly suggested an expedition that would take us out of the sequestered precincts of the tourist hotel and into the cluster of impoverished little huts she had until now so carefully avoided.

"It's not very far," Mao Hua said, pointing down a small alley that lead through a labyrinth of tiny houses and courtyards.

We walked in silence to the Tower of Questions, savouring the sounds and smells of the little community through which we passed, the last emblems of our time together: the cries of mothers scolding their children, the aroma of cooking rice and fried bread, the guarded invitations issued by painted doors opening just a crack onto small private courtyards.

An elderly woman sat by the stairs of the tower. She sang a peasant song at the top of her old and cracking voice, a song about suffering and joy, feast and famine, and hopes for a plentiful harvest. At first, we thought she had been hired to take tickets, but before we handed her our small stubs of paper, she waved us on with a gesture of her hand and a wide, toothless grin.

We began our ascent, Mao Hua leading and I following behind. The tower had nine tiers. We climbed slowly and methodically, Mao Hua insisting that we stop for a while at each tier to savour the view. On the first tier, we could see over the roofs of the tiny houses in the compound to the nearby fields. By the third one, the rice paddies at the edge of the city came into view. At the top, we beheld the whole of the surrounding countryside. All China lay before us. I turned with excitement to Mao Hua, but her eyes were like stones. We stood in silence for a while then circled around the upper tier of the tower.

At last, Mao Hua spoke. "Sometimes I wonder what will happen to me." She stopped and turned to face the open fields.

"What are you thinking?" I asked.

"Perhaps I am praying."

"Praying to whom?"

"To the god of Klee Wyck," she answered with a sudden smile.

It was a warm day for early November in the north, and the sun was shining bountifully on the rice paddies below, transforming them into an undulating sea of green. A slight haze enveloped the scene in an ethereal magic, lending it all the luminosity of an impressionist painting. The sadness had not passed, but it had been buried again. As we stood there, Klee Wyck and I, on the topmost tier of the Wenfeng Tower, I wanted to ask her if from where she stood she could see the pattern that connected all things.

Gone to Shenzhen

SHENZHEN, THE SPECIAL Economic Zone flanked by the South China Sea, right next to Hong Kong, was a place spoken of often by my students as a Chinese Shangri-La, an oasis of freedom on the edge of a vast desert, and a door to the world beyond.

In Shenzhen, Mr. Tan told me, you could become rich overnight. It was warm there, with palm trees and the blue sea stretching before you. And if you could speak English, it was easy to meet some foreign friends who would hire you for work abroad.

But none of us really knew much about Shenzhen. No one had personally known anyone who had gone there, except Madame Liu, and her perceptions were biased, since her only daughter had moved there to work in a glass factory. Even more than a Shangri-La, to Madame Liu Shenzhen was a place of happy reunion with her daughter every second spring. Overflowing with enthusiasm about the place, she had shown me albums filled with pictures of her visits there. But to me, Shenzhen looked like any other place in southern China.

The night Mr. Tan left us, I was competing in the university's annual song contest, one of the many midwinter diversions thought of by my students to fill up the bitterly cold, empty weeks following the Spring Festival vacation in January. Miss Tian Xiaonan and I had made it to the final round of the contest. As the students huddled together in the unheated Student Union Building, we strutted across the stage in heavy makeup and gold scarves singing one of the latest pop hits from Taiwan, "Hua Ji" ("Lamentation of the Flowers"), by a singer named Qi Qin. About the sorrow of separation, the song began with the lines, "Why are you leaving now that it is spring? Won't you stay and walk with me a while?"

Afterwards I asked Miss Tian if she wanted to sing for a living. She replied, "Oh yes, I plan to go to Shenzhen and become a rock star."

I got back to the guest-house late. I assumed Mr. Tan had already gone home. I didn't hear the news until morning: in a world in which jobs were almost impossible to lose or change, Mr. Tan had been fired.

"What was the reason?" I asked Lao Zheng, who just nodded his head, closed his Buddha eyes, and smiled.

I asked around for more information. Everyone knew Mr. Tan had been fired, but no one knew where he had gone. Weeks passed and I heard nothing from Mr. Tan. Instead, I received news from Ding Liang. Fed up with life at the small teachers' college where he worked, Ding Liang had taken off one night, leaving behind a note saying he had gone to his parents' home in a distant town to recuperate from an illness. In fact, he had gone to Shenzhen.

Ding Liang had spent several glorious weeks in Shenzhen before returning, suspiciously, with a tan. Ding wasn't planning to stay in his small town in the north of the province, he confided to me in his letter. If he returned to Shenzhen, he had been promised a job selling brushes for a company that would send him to Hungary.

A month later I met Mr. Fu at a dance party in the new nightclub in town. The foreign teachers had been invited to dance the opening waltzes. One of Mr. Tan's closest friends, Mr. Fu seemed a good source of information about him.

"Oh, Mr. Tan has gone to Shenzhen," Mr. Fu said when I asked.

"Shenzhen?" I repeated.

"Yes, to work for a foreign company."

"What wonderful news! Please tell him to write to me."

Months passed and I still hadn't heard from Mr. Tan. Then one day I ran into his sister in a local department store. "How is Mr. Tan?" I asked.

"Oh, he is fine," she replied.

"How does he like Shenzhen?"

"Shenzhen?" she repeated, puzzled.

"Isn't he in Shenzhen?"

"No, he is here in Hefei still looking for work."

The next time I saw Mr. Fu I confronted him. "Why did you tell me Mr. Tan was in Shenzhen?"

"Oh, I am so sorry," Mr. Fu apologized, "but Mr. Tan did not want you to know he had no job. He wanted to save face. And he knew you would be proud of him if you thought he had gone to Shenzhen."

I thanked Mr. Fu for telling me the truth at last and rode away on my bicycle.

I never did see Mr. Tan again. He preferred to sacrifice our friendship rather than lose face. As for Miss Tian Xiaonan, she didn't become a rock star in Shenzhen but a teacher in her home town in the countryside, and as Ding Liang wrote me much later, as far as Hungary went, he preferred China.

When I returned to visit China the next year, I asked after two of my graduate students, Miss Zhang and Miss Ju. On graduation, both students had been given the best possible job assignment: teaching in the Foreign Languages

Department at our university. "How are they?" I asked a former colleague.

"Oh, I wouldn't know," she replied. "They have gone to Shenzhen."

I walked through the campus back to the guest-house. It was a year later, but the same music was still blasting out of the windows of the student dormitory. I recognized the song Miss Tian Xiaonan had sung with me at the university singing contest: "Why are you going now that the flowers are about to bloom? Won't you stay and walk with me a while?"

Wu Jiao's Hand

I FIRST MET WU JIAO in the campus store a few weeks before the annual school track meet, which took place in early October. I was buying a tin container for carrying my dinner vegetables home from the teachers' cafeteria, a kind of white mess tin that had the name of our university written in Mao Zedong's hand on one side and a number, sixty-eight, on the other. As I looked up from examining the mess tin, I saw Wu Jiao's face, and from that day on, every time I held out my tin for a scoop of dinner vegetables, I thought of Wu Jiao's hand, of the way he wrote his name and mine in Chinese characters with that tender, uncertain scrawl.

The head coach in the Physical Training Department, Wu Jiao was thirty years old and still unmarried, though he had a casual girlfriend, a second-year student who adored him. His bachelorhood puzzled the middle-aged matrons who served as the self-appointed guardians of the morals of the community. What was Wu Jiao waiting for, they wondered, a miracle from heaven?

About three weeks before the track meet, Wu Jiao visited my rooms with Gu Jie, one of my Shakespeare students. Wu Jiao had a novel idea, Gu Jie explained: why didn't I enter the teachers' race? It would be historical for one of the foreign teachers to take part in the race, he continued excitedly, and who would be a better coach than Wu Jiao? Would I consider it? In high school, I had been a prize-winning sprinter, but I hadn't run in years.

"But Mr. Wu will help you,"Gu Jie insisted.

"All right," I agreed. "But is there anything I can do for Mr. Wu?" I asked in an effort to reciprocate.

"If you could improve Mr. Wu's English, even a little," said Gu Jie after talking things over in Chinese with the uncomprehending Wu, "Mr. Wu would never forget you."

Our daily training began after classes were over for the day. I would run from my graduate seminar in Shakespeare to the playing field; Wu Jiao would saunter over to meet me after putting Cao Meihua through the paces of her general fitness test. At the university, Physical Education was compulsory, and each student had to maintain a certain level of basic physical fitness to keep a passing grade. Cao Meihua, a studious but unathletic person, could never manage to get through the required number of sit-ups and laps around the track. One day, Cao Meihua came to me in tears and begged me to write a note excusing her from Physical Education on the pretence that she was doing research for me on Shakespeare. After she was exempted, Wu Jiao had even more time and energy for my own training.

Wu Jiao and I usually trained until well after dark. I ran around the track while Wu Jiao watched, timing me. He made me practise my starts and finishes, and taught me how to pace myself and how to stretch beforehand and afterwards so I wouldn't strain or pull any muscles. Since I spoke only a little Chinese and Wu hardly any English, we communicated through gestures and body language of the most ridiculous sort. That was Wu's workout. As for my own, Wu's goal was to do a complete overhaul, to make me into a finely tuned machine, primed for performance on the day of the race.

Our training carried through to the Mid-autumn Festival. In the autumn of the year in Hefei, just before winter sets in, there is a sadness in the air, not because the leaves are falling or the air turns sharp and poignant with the scent of the passing year, but because the stars begin to grow bright and cold. When you look up at them, you are reminded of the King of Heaven and his seven daughters. One of the daughters fell in love with a cowherd and stole away to live on earth, forfeiting her place in the starry firmament for a time until her father discovered her secret love and banished her from earth forever, leaving her a faintly shimmering star, broken-hearted and crystalline, and the cowherd bereft, with no reason for living. But the King of Heaven eventually took pity on the two lovers and allowed them to meet once a year on the seventh day of the seventh lunar month. On that day, all the magpies in the world form a bridge upon which husband and wife meet. On the remaining days of the year, they live on opposite sides of the Silver River, recognizable to all as the stars Altair and Vega.

In his own pantomimed way, Wu Jiao conveyed the main points of this story of thwarted love as we cycled home from the playing field at twilight. In exchange, I told him, in my faltering Chinese interspersed with a smattering of English, the myth of Diana, the goddess of the moon, and of Venus, the goddess of love. Wu Jiao liked the myth of Venus best. Afterwards, whenever some problem came up, he would say with confidence, "Venus will help me!" Wu Jiao believed in love as the Buddhist believes in nirvana: it was something to aspire to always, and, once attained, days of blissful happiness would be yours.

Wu Jiao and Gu Jie lived too far from home to visit their families during the Mid-autumn Festival, so they decided to celebrate the occasion by taking in a film at the local cinema, and they asked me to come along. The day before the festival, I received two gifts: a package of crisp watermelon mooncakes from the dean of the Foreign Languages Department and a gold scarf made of a glittering synthetic fabric, from a mystery visitor to the guest-house. When Gu Jie saw me, he immediately complimented me on the scarf. Wu Jiao said nothing, but I did notice him glance at it from time to time with a strange vague kind of longing.

We cycled downtown, with Wu Jiao on the outside, next to the passing traffic, and Gu Jie next to me. Gu Jie, who usually did the talking for both himself and Wu Jiao, explained to me that Wu had deliberately placed himself in the position of greatest risk for the sake of protecting me. I really didn't understand why Gu Jie was telling me this or why Wu Jiao was doing it, but I assumed it must have something to with the responsibility Wu Jiao felt as my coach to safeguard my physical well-being.

We arrived at the cinema early, so we went across the street to Connie's Café, where we sat for half an hour imbibing rock music, cigarette smoke, hot milk made from milk powder, and a kind of sickly sweet white cake that might have been served in Woolworth's sometime in the 1950s before the health-food craze began. I had to admit the cake was delicious.

As we ate, we chatted about the track meet. Should I enter the race, Wu Jiao wondered, under my English name or under one of my Chinese names? Wu didn't think Hu Jinle (Happy Silk) sounded like the name of a track star; he preferred Xu Yazhu (Graceful Bamboo). Still, he liked any name better than the transliteration of my English name used by my colleagues, Ha Qisen (Laughing in a Beautiful Jade Forest). Gu Jie thought any name would do, but preferred a Chinese one. After all, he said, this was China and all of us were trying in our own way to contribute to the motherland. In the end, we decided I would enter the race as Hu Jinle.

The movie was in Hindi, with Chinese voice-over and English subtitles. About the triumph of the family over those forces that threaten its well-being—egotism, professional ambition, and the wayward impulses of the human heart in general—the film was what a student of Shakespeare would call a romance. Gu Jie was the best of the four graduate students in my Shakespeare seminar. We were studying *Othello* at the time, which he liked much better than *Romeo and Juliet*, he told me, because *Othello* was about a real-life dilemma and dealt with interesting things, like madness and obsession. He didn't want me to get him wrong, he said. *Romeo and Juliet* was also a great play, but when you looked at it closely, it was just about love. Why couldn't Romeo and Juliet just do the sensible thing and obey their parents? "*That* is the question," Gu Jie said, echoing his favourite play by Shakespeare.

Gu Jie found the Hindi film silly and sentimental, preferring the initial government propaganda on breast cancer with its dramatized instructions for breast self-examination, since it was educational. Wu Jiao didn't say much, but his eyes glistened at the end of the film when the man and woman ran in slow motion, together with their two children, through a field of flowers as sentimental music played in the background.

Outside the cinema, we munched on candy-covered crab apples, then rode home. By the campus fishpond, we all wished on a star. I wished that Gu Jie and Wu Jiao would realize their most cherished dreams, in this way leaving a blank slot for them to fill in in the privacy of their own thoughts. Gu Jie wished that I would find happiness in China, again leaving a blank space. But Wu Jiao wished that I would be like Diana, as mysterious as the moon.

"And oh, by the way," Gu Jie added with significance, "the film was compliments of Mr. Wu."

The day of the track meet dawned gritty and grey. The air that morning seemed especially heavy with the coal dust that blackens Chinese lungs and fills up the sanitoriums of the country. Wu Jiao arrived at dawn for my early morning workout. As we went through my paces, I could see that, despite all my training, he had no confidence in me at all. Still, we played out our charade, and with a quick hand-shake, Wu Jiao left me at the guest-house to change into my track clothes, a pair of black Lycra leggings and a sweat-shirt with the name of our university inscribed on it in Mao Zedong's hand.

As I dressed for the meet, I contemplated that hand. If you place a letter of the Roman alphabet beside a Chinese character, you immediately see the difference. While the Roman letter stands there boldly saying everything, the Chinese character, with its lines and boxes inside lines and boxes, implies a myriad of things yet is loathe to reveal any-thing at all. But if you study it, it speaks. Mao Zedong's hand, for example, was subtle but strong, refined yet bold. Idly, I wondered what Wu Jiao's hand was like.

At nine o'clock, a local Communist Party official from the Provincial Education Bureau officially opened the track meet. He talked about the founding of the university, telling the story of how Mao himself had visited it and inscribed its name in his own hand, causing it to flourish even to this day. My race was the very first. The starting gun sounded and we all took off around the track.

I was doing far better than Wu Jiao could have ever expected. I was at least twenty paces ahead of Miss Hao, the teacher who won the race every year and was a legend around campus for her fleetness of foot. I maintained my lead the whole eight hundred metres and broke through the finish line and into a crowd of students shouting "Jia-you! Jia-you!" (Go! Go!) at the top of their lungs. I col-lapsed into their arms with joy and relief. Miss Hao sped by me. I noticed she wasn't slowing down or being comforted by her most loyal students. She was passing me by, running at full tilt, her black cropped hair blowing in the gritty wind and her lithe, wiry body taut to the muscle.

How could I have known it was a thousand-metre run,

not an eight hundred? Wu Jiao had only his bad English to blame. He stood beside me now, gesticulating wildly. I understood that he wanted me to keep running and overtake Miss Hao. I picked myself up and ran. Miss Hao was about a hundred metres ahead of me by now, but still I ran.

I came in a respectable third, and at the end of the day I was called up along with the other two winning teachers to the raised platforms to be honoured by the Master of Ceremonies. "Third place," the voice called out in Chinese over the loudspeaker, "Hu Jinle!" Everyone cheered as Professor Jiang pinned the blue ribbon on my sweatshirt and handed me a very large thermos for my boiled drinking water. Afterwards, Wu Jiao sauntered onto the field and posed for a photo with me, and then for another with Gu Jie and myself.

There were three things the students remembered about the day: how Professor Pang fell backwards off the spectators' stand and almost broke his back; how Miss Zhu, the student track star, collapsed as she crossed the finish line for the long-distance run and was taken to her dormitory room unconscious; and how Hu Jinle, the foreign teacher, finished third in a race she could easily have won.

Wu Jiao took the whole thing stoically. But as I found out a few weeks later when I took my first trip alone in China, the track meet and my running abilities no longer held the same importance for him. In the course of my training, our friendship had been transmuted from copper to pure gold.

I had been in China barely three months. My command of Chinese was still basic, but with some pantomime I could usually manage to convey my meaning. Whether that meaning was understood once conveyed was another thing, but still I had come to the point where my students felt I could travel alone. And so I decided to book a train ticket to Shanghai to visit Heping, who had been a visiting scholar at my university in Canada.

No foreigners' seats—"soft-seats," as they are called—

were available. It was an overnight trip, and I was not used to China so I needed a seat where I could lie down and rest, my students argued, discussing the problem among themselves. It was enough that I was going to Shanghai alone. I should take one thing at a time. Then one morning very early, Gu Jie came to my door and handed me a soft-seat ticket to Shanghai. Had I not insisted, he wouldn't have even let me pay for it, though he would have considered the price of the ticket exorbitant. He told me he had made all the arrangements for my departure: he and Qu Ruiying would see me off on Friday night. "How will I get to the station?" I asked. Someone would take me there, he assured me.

On Friday night, I stood by the guest-house gate waiting for someone to come and take me to the station. With two transfers of buses, the trip could take as much as an hour. I was getting worried that I would miss my train when Wu Jiao rode up on his bicycle.

Trying to speak colloquially, he said, "Hope on!"

"What?" I asked.

"Hope on!" he repeated.

Finally, I understood: Wu Jiao was asking me to "hop on" to his bicycle so he could take me to the station. I had no choice. I hopped on and tried to distract myself by counting the cracks in the pavement as we rode down the bumpy, dusty road from the east gate of the university to the city centre. Several times, I fell off the carrier at the back or had to get off. Relative to me, Wu Jiao was slight, and transporting not only me but a bulging overnight bag and a cloth purse filled with gifts for Heping and his family all the way to the centre of the city was obviously taxing his endurance to the limits. By the time we approached the station, the moon had emerged, bright and evanescent, from behind violet clouds. I thought of Diana, of Venus, and then of Wu Jiao, whose forehead was soaked with perspiration, despite the coolness of the November evening.

At the train station, Wu Jiao shooed me into the

Foreigners' Waiting Room. To my surprise, Qu Ruiying and Gu Jie calmly waited for me there. Wu Jiao sat me down, and before I could thank him he had disappeared. Qu Ruiying and Gu Jie continued to sit, waiting with complete composure to see me off. A voice came over the PA system, and they rose from their seats, each grabbing a piece of my luggage.

Gu Jie and Qu Ruiying studied my soft-seat ticket closely. They counted the cars, asked for directions, then counted them again. They lifted my bags up onto the train. I followed passively. They looked for my compartment. I trailed wordlessly behind. They tucked my belongings into the space under the seat. I sat in the assigned place. Qu Ruiying was the first to leave the compartment. When she had gone, Gu Jie reached into his jacket pocket.

"I have something for you," he said. "It's a letter. You may read it after I have gone. Good luck!" Then he, too, disappeared.

The train pulled out of the station. Qu Ruiying and Gu Jie hovered outside my window. Qu waved a white handkerchief in a kind of longing gesture she must have seen in the movies. Gu Jie stood at attention; waving was beneath his dignity. As the train pulled away, Hefei faded into the darkness of a distant world, the safe cocoon around which Gu Jie, Qu Ruiying, and Wu Jiao spun their concern, protecting me from all harm. I was completely alone now in China.

I settled into my soft-seat, smiled and nodded at the Chinese passengers across from me in response to their smiles and nods, then pulled out Wu Jiao's letter. I opened it and read: "You know I love you pretty much. And so Mr. Gu suggested me to ask for your hand."

Was Wu Jiao really proposing marriage? I didn't know whether to be flattered or annoyed. The letter was written in bad English, probably by Wu Jiao himself. It read:

. . . Why do I wish to study abroad and coach? I think that I explain three programs:

111

1) Position: Like our teachers in our China it's not a social position. We are not respected by people. This hurts our feelings. So the world is coming to the dog.

2) Economic: Because our teacher isn't a social position. Our salaries glue our mouth.

3) Life aid: The fields of research is to elaborate the technical and tactical principle of playing table tennis from the angle of physiological psychology. But our Chinese researching is pretty poor and latest, so I want to go to America to study advanced sports psychology. . . .

Maybe it is not polite for me to point this question. The latest difficulty is to find a sponsor for me. If this question is solved so I will be abroad to make my dream of life as early as possible but I will come back to save our Chinese people. So I want you to ask your friends in U.S.A. to help me in this "sponsor question." But if you have any difficulty, it's none of your business. Also I will help you forever. If you can help, please telegraph from my dear Shanghai. Take care! . . .

There followed, in Chinese characters, Wu Jiao's name.

I examined the characters. The hand was wobbly and unsure, yet somehow confident and bold. It was the hand of someone who had played his last card and gambled away his last cent. I didn't telegraph Wu Jiao. I couldn't think of anyone who would be willing to sponsor him. Besides, didn't Wu Jiao know I was a Canadian, not an American? Still, it was a letter from a friend, so I put it in my pocket and carried it there the whole weekend as a kind of talisman to protect me in a foreign land.

In Shanghai, the weather was unseasonably warm for November. I wandered the Mandarin Gardens eating a street-fried breaded egg, a specialty of the old city. I cycled with my friend Heping and walked along the Bund with the children. I even had my photo taken in front of the fountain across the street from the Peace Hotel. By the time the train pulled into Hefei on Sunday night, the weather had turned cold again. I dreaded finding my own way home on such a bitter night. I left my comfortable soft-seat car for the grey, dirty station and moved with the heavy stream of people flowing through the ticket stamper's gate. All around me, passengers were being met by relatives, friends, and business associates. Some held signs with Chinese characters inscribed on them. It was cold and late; still, one of the university drivers had been sent to get me. I waved and pushed my way through the crowd to his car. We drove back through the dark, cold city to the university campus.

The lights in the teachers' dormitories were out and the guest-house was quiet. Even Lao Zheng had gone to bed. I hadn't expected anyone to receive me; it was too late and there were 7:30 classes the next morning. I crawled through an open window then tiptoed down the hall to my rooms. As I did, I thought about Wu Jiao. I wondered if he would avoid me from now on, embarrassed that his bold request for help had been rejected.

As I put the key into the lock, I saw a small piece of paper tucked under the door. I picked it up and read: "Mr. Gu and Miss Qu and me, we waited you, then the gates locked. Welcome to home, Hu Jinle!" The English was recognizable and so were the Chinese characters inscribed at the bottom of the page in that tender, uncertain scrawl. I saw Wu the next day and the day after that. Over the course of the year, Wu Jiao's English improved a little. We became good friends and spoke of many things. But neither of us ever mentioned the letter Wu Jiao had written asking for my hand.

THE TIES THAT BIND

"Guanxi, guanxi, everything that exists has guanxi," lamented Zhou Bin as he downed his third glass of maotai. *A slick and ambitious young bureaucrat assigned to preside over the affairs of the foreign teachers, Zhou, our official liaison with the Foreign Affairs Office, seemed strangely out of character. As he slumped over the table with a comic grin on his face, he looked more like one of Shakespeare's sage and open-hearted jesters than a Communist Party official. A tragicomic figure both in real life and in his Shakespearean aspect of the moment, like all of Shakespeare's jesters, Zhou Bin spoke the truth.*

*"Connections"—*guanxi *is an essential part of Chinese life. Without* guanxi, *you can do nothing. With* guanxi, *anything is possible. For example, in order to get a train ticket without getting up at dawn and lining up for hours, you have to have a friend in the ticketing office; and if you know a ticketing agent for Air China, you can buy tickets on flights that are officially sold out. A highly placed university official, whose daughter would soon be going to Canada and wished to be introduced to my friends there, was able to bring me in only twenty-four hours a small box of goods*

that had been held up for weeks in customs in Nanjing. And it was guanxi *that made the official university drivers two of the most powerful people on campus. Everyone needed a car to go somewhere. I will never forget Wu Li's story: having insufficient* guanxi *to get a driver, her husband had to wheel her on a wooden cart to the hospital for the delivery of her child.*

In China, the business of forming relationships really is a business. And cultivating relationships is the essence of Chinese life. My students often tried such tactics with me. They brought me presents, invited me to their homes, and took me on outings. Colleagues did the same. I accepted gratefully, thinking the Chinese the warmest and most hospitable people I had ever known. It was not untrue. But until I learned about the Confucian ethic of reciprocity, an ethic still alive and well in communist China, I was taken aback when I inevitably received a request, usually for a recommendation, or for sponsorship to study abroad. After a while, I understood that guanxi, *like gossip, the favourite national pastime, is a fact of Chinese life accepted by most though disliked by many.*

What is the meaning of guanxi? *I think at the heart of the system of reciprocal relationships that each person erects around him or herself is the belief that nobody should be left alone, that community is the ultimate good, and that no one has the right to live for himself. "No man is an island"—my undergraduate students loved to quote these words of John Donne to me, and when they did, they uttered them with a conviction sufficient to sway even the sceptic. They could see I knew nothing about their philosophy of life. I did what I liked when I liked, without consulting anyone. Foreigners, they must have thought, were unpredictable.*

As for me, it took a long time to learn the complex dance of relationships I had unwittingly taken up simply by virtue of living in China. It was anything but a two-step, the only step I had fully mastered after months of attendance at university dance parties. Relationships were an intricate tango of cordialities and convivialities, of thoughtfulness in word but mostly in deed. Was it wrong to barter in deeds rather than in words, as North Americans do? Deeds went deeper, I thought.

By the end of my time in China, I had forged ties stronger than guanxi, *truly sacrificial relationships in which little was asked and much was given simply for the sake of friendship, a cardinal value in Chinese society. "May our friendship be as long as the Yangtze River," officials toasted me at banquets. "I will always remember you," my friends told me at moments of deepest intimacy. "Never forget me," they exhorted me on separation.*

For many of my friends, the thought of their erasure from my consciousness caused intense pain. The ties that bind were always to be remembered. Like history, they were to be kept eternally present in the mind. Even guanxi, *I began to see, was more than tit for tat: it reflected the simple truth that the human family is intimately connected by the business of life.*

Darling

"I TAKE YOU SHOPPING!" says Daoling, with pearly white teeth flashing a broad grin.

"I have no money," I reply.

"Have! Have!" says Daoling, pulling out a thick wad of *yuan.* "Don't worry anything."

"But I can't take your money," I protest.

"Pay back," she says. "Pay back sometime. Don't worry anything!"

At the first silk shop we pass, Daoling stops. She pulls me inside. Chatters in Chinese with the clerk, a young girl about twenty who is totally disinterested in me and my purchases. Within five minutes, Daoling has her running back and forth, showering me with silk pyjamas—pink, white, cream. Silk shirts, silk jackets, silk everything.

"Large size!" I hear her commanding the clerk in Chinese. "Very large size!"

Daoling stands a petite five foot one. Bangs. Short black hair. Perfect teeth. Pearly white. Mother of one son. Nuclear scientist. Member of Academia Sinica. Leading researcher in her field. I stand five foot nine. Awkward. Tall. Blonde. Freckle-faced. A foreigner. Crowds gather around me. Discuss me. They wonder, "How did she get here? Who is the Chinese lady? What do you think of that white blouse? Does it suit or not?"

While I try on the white silk blouse, a crowd gathers. Each person discusses me, my choice. I waver. Some step in. Each makes his or her own bid. In Chinese. In broken English. Others smile indulgently, following carefully every detail of the discussion.

"How much is it?" I ask Daoling, who has settled on one with a round neck and leg-of-mutton sleeves.

"Only a few Canadian dollars," she answers.

"How many yuan?" I ask Daoling.

"One hundred and fifty."

"So expensive!"

"No matter. No matter. Only a few Canadian dollars. Take! Take!" She pulls out a wad of bills and then pays the cashier, who packages the silk blouse.

Satisfied, the crowd begins to disperse, still discussing things: "Did you see that foreigner buying the white silk blouse? She is a teacher from Hefei. Blonde hair. White doesn't suit at all. Need red. Bright colour."

We continue down Nanjing Road, striking out again and again. No clothes large enough for a very tall blonde foreigner. This is not the tourist section but where the Chinese shop. No large sizes. Just Chinese sizes.

Shanghai's Number One Department Store comes into view. It's almost Christmas, but no lights, no displays. This is China. No Christmas here. Only Daoling.

We enter the store, pass racks of exquisite sweaters, all colours, designs, and styles. Angora, mohair, wool. Aisle after aisle, floor to ceiling.

"You like?" Daoling asks, taking me on a tour of the floor.

"Maybe," I answer.

I choose one or two. We ask if there is a large size.

There is none. Choose another. Ask. Yes, there is. I try it on.

"Take! Take!" Daoling cries. "Only a few Canadian dollars." She pulls out a wad of bills.

In every section of the store, it is the same: "Take! Take! . . . Large size."

I add a pair of brown lace-up boots to my repertoire. They make me think of the boots Anne of Green Gables might have worn as she waited in the train station for her adoptive parents. Sturdy, unflattering, and slightly pathetic.

"Don't worry. You need," Daoling says. "Only a few Canadian dollars!"

Next she grabs a pair of exquisite white silk pyjamas. "For your wedding night," she explains as she brings out her wad of bills and pays the clerk.

Silk jacket. "Take." Angora sweater. "Take." Silk dress. "Take."

I ask, "How will I carry all this home?"

On the third floor we pass through the luggage section. Daoling says, "Suitcase. Take. Only a few Canadian dollars." She pulls out her wad of bills.

Silk shirt. Silk jacket. All fit well into the large black suitcase with wheels and a strap.

Daoling and I climb up the stairs to the overpass outside the Shanghai Number One Department Store. For blocks, the lights of Nanjing Road sparkle. Almost like Christmas.

Daoling asks shyly, "Take my picture?"

I snap a shot of Daoling posing on the overpass, with the brightly coloured lights of the city flashing behind her. Her eyes are shining and her pearly white teeth glistening.

Then Daoling asks to take my picture. As she does, she admonishes me: "Smile! Don't worry anything. Be happy! Be happy! Don't worry anything!"

Daoling and I descend the stairs to the street. Together, we pull the bulging suitcase down Nanjing Road. As we do, I say half to her, half to myself, "Thank you, Darling!"

A Confucian Scholar

"I DON'T THINK YOU will survive another year," said Professor Y. K. Wang. "It does not seem to be a reasonable option."

I coughed a little, my bronchitis betraying me. Perhaps Professor Wang imagined me ending up in the sanitorium right next door to the campus. The thought had crossed my mind in recent days. Why wasn't the infection clearing up? At the hospital, the doctor had given me every root, berry, and leaf he could think of. He may have even thrown in the dust from a few deer antlers and a ground-up monkey's paw. And yet it had not helped. Maybe what I needed was some good Western antibiotics, if there were any to be had. There weren't.

"One of my students in America made the same mistake," Professor Wang continued. "She left her country not knowing how Chinese she really was. Perhaps you don't know how much you belong to your own country?"

Forgetting me almost entirely now, Professor Wang began to reminisce: "You know, all my brightest students

121

have gone to America, and all of them keep in touch. Each one writes at least once a year. For example, Tang Yan . . ." He walked towards his desk, pulled open a drawer, and took out some pictures. "Ph.D., English literature," he mused. "University of Maryland."

Professor Wang paused for a moment. "She speaks English almost perfectly. But only 'almost.' No non-native speaker can ever capture the accent fully. I am convinced of that. In fact, I know from personal experience," he said with a nod of his head.

I looked around the room at the vast library of books lining the walls: English grammar books, books of English idioms, the classics of English literature, lexicons, dictionaries. The books gave their own silent testimony.

"When I studied in Shanghai many decades ago," Professor Y. K. Wang continued, "China was a different world. Now we have a lot more just–ice." He pronounced the word forcefully, stressing the first syllable. "Yes, the Party has done a lot of good for the people. You see, socialism with 'Chinese characteristics,'" he said, emphasizing the word *Chinese.*

"And the future?" I asked. "Who does the future belong to?"

Professor Y. K. Wang thought for a moment. "You know," he said, "the Japanese are a superior race. A very superior race. The Chinese could learn a great deal from them, especially the capacity to work as a group. And the Germans, they are an intellectual race. The Chinese . . . the poor Chinese. At the present time, they are a very backward race. . . ." Then, suddenly, an idea seemed to light up his face and he added, "The Chinese, the Chinese have turned away from their traditional values. They do not know themselves anymore. They have lost the capacity for self-knowledge. Yes, that is it: it is self-knowledge they lack."

"And the students?" I asked.

"Yes," he nodded, "the future belongs to the students.

We support them. They will lead the way as the rest of us falter due to senile decay." I could hear the music of the rain as it fell on the *ba-jiao* leaves outside the window. It made a mournful sound, almost a cry, the cry of one who was very far away from home. It was a cold afternoon in March, one of the many seemingly empty afternoons on the quiet campus. No sounds or stirrings of life anywhere. It was the kind of afternoon on which no warmth could be found in an unheated Chinese apartment and no interest in life except that generated by the conversation between an aging Confucian scholar and an ailing foreign teacher as they mused over two precious glasses of hot milk made from milk powder. "No, you will never survive another year," Professor Wang concluded, signalling that the conversation was over and it was time for me to go home.

The pronouncement rang in the cold air like a bell. I thought of Tang Yan puttering around her apartment in a distant land, far away from her campus home here in China. No matter how homesick she got, no matter how ill she might become, she would stay to honour Professor Y. K. Wang's confidence in her abilities as a scholar. She would sacrifice everything for what she thought was a better education and a better life, exchanging her sonorous, musical Mandarin for a faltering English that would never be quite perfect.

I looked across the room at Professor Y. K. Wang. Above his head, on the wall, hung a piece of calligraphy, bold and beautiful. I wondered if the verse was from Confucius. I remembered another saying, attributed to Confucius, that I had seen carved in stone near the entranceway of a university in Shanghai: "Seek the truth. Cultivate originality. Live up to the name of teacher."

I rose to leave. "You know, it's just a cold," I said to Professor Wang. "It has nothing to do with China. And whether I stay or go, you will always be my teacher."

Exchanging Pictures

WHENEVER CHINESE STUDENTS want to show friendship towards you, they give you their picture, and it is expected that you will give them one in return. The best kind is of you in a People's Liberation Army uniform. That's standard. But a winsome pose with face framed by the branch of a weeping willow is also acceptable for a woman. The woman should have one of her fingers touching the end of the branch. And a man should be looking far off into the distance in front of a well-known public monument, or crouching on the steps of a newly built highrise, which in Hefei means any building from two to fourteen storeys tall. In Chinese, there is a special word for a building that has more than one floor, *loufang*.

I remember the photo of Li Xiaohua, a young woman introduced to me by a Canadian friend. That was before I lived in China. She had been corresponding with my friend, who warned me that Li had become rather dependent on her. Apparently, Li viewed my friend as her adoptive Canadian mother and expected everything from her. It didn't sound encouraging, but Li was living close to the city where I would be teaching. I didn't know anyone there. I thought it might be nice to get to know her, and Li obviously felt the same way. Perhaps she thought it would be good insurance to have two Canadian friends to depend on. I wrote to her and she replied. The letter was short, but inside was a small snapshot in black and white of a delicately pretty young woman. On the back was written, "From your true friend, Li Xiaohua." In order to be appropriately reciprocal, I sent Li a recent graduation photo of myself inscribed in kind.

It was months before I corresponded with Li again. Once I had arrived in China, I was consumed by my duties as one of four foreign teachers sparsely spread over several thousand students, all of them eager to learn English. The Taxation Bureau where Li worked as an accountant was in the town of Lu'an, not far away. Perhaps she could come to the university in Hefei sometime to see me? I wrote and asked. I didn't hear from Li for weeks. Then one Saturday, late in November, there came an insistent knock on my door. I wasn't expecting any visitors, and I had asked Lao Zheng to ward off any students. Dressed in the turquoise silk housecoat I had bought in Hangzhou, I was trying to make myself comfortable as I settled in for a long night of marking student papers.

"It's Dean Qi," the voice called out from the other side of the door. "There is someone here to see you," he said.

"Could they come back later?" I asked as I pulled my housecoat tightly around me and hurriedly gathered up the piles of student papers from the floor.

"I don't think so," he replied. "You had better open the door."

I threw on my khaki pants and a T-shirt and opened the door. Beside Dean Qi stood a young woman and her friend. "This girl says she knows you," the dean said sceptically. The young woman was not pretty in a conventional sense; in fact, she looked rather homely. Her voice was low.

She was stockily built, and she swayed nervously from side to side as she entered my room. The very essence of self-consciousness, she wouldn't raise her eyes to meet mine or speak a single word. Not even my name or her own could get past her lips. To add to the dean's chagrin, every time he addressed her she broke into a fit of embarrassed giggles.

After about five minutes of this, Dean Qi finally interjected, "She says you sent her this postcard, and she has your picture. She came to my house and showed it to me, asking if I could help her find you." I could tell that the dean was losing his patience with the awkward girl. He seemed anxious to excuse himself as soon as gracefully possible. At his prompting, the young woman, eyes still downcast, held up a battered postcard and a well-worn picture of me. I read the inscription on the back: it was Li Xiaohua.

Li Xiaohua looked nothing like the picture she had sent me. She was ten years older than the girl in the snapshot. And instead of the frail and delicate appearance of that young girl, she had the sturdy physique of a peasant woman whose labours had worn away her girlish form. During the whole time she stood in my living room, Li Xiaohua never did get out a word. I invited Li and her friend to dinner, but they nodded their heads in refusal. Maybe they had something else to do? So I walked the two of them to the campus gates. The least I could do was see them off.

The dean had already made his escape. After several attempts at making conversation, I, too, was ready to say goodbye. But as I reached out to shake her hand in farewell, Li seized the last moment of her chance.

"I've never talked to a foreigner before," she blurted out, "but I am so happy to meet you." She spoke with the slightest trace of a British accent.

"Next time we will have dumplings together," I replied, relieved that she had spoken at last.

Li Xiaohua never said another word to me, and I never saw her or heard from her again.

Sun Li's First Flight

IT IS NOT EASY TO GET an air ticket in China. Sometimes you have to haggle for hours. Or you have to come back the next day. Sometimes you are told there are no more seats. But if you know someone who can help you, you find that suddenly there is a seat, the last seat on the plane, and it's yours—the very last seat on any flight to anywhere, be it Urumqi or Guilin.

In China, *guanxi*, or "connections," is the axis around which life turns. Though the word refers to something quite indefinable, you can't do anything without it. *Guanxi* is, at once, nothing and everything. It is, at heart, a contradiction.

It was the end of April, and since my teaching job in Hefei would soon be over, I was flying to Beijing for a job interview. A colleague had introduced me to the dean of the Foreign Languages Department at one of the city's major universities, and I hoped he would offer me a contract to teach English there the following year. A student whose mother's neighbour's friend worked in the ticket

127

office had purchased the ticket for me. I was cowering inside the door of the ticket office, shielding myself from the damp April breeze, when Sun Li approached. Sun Li was late for work. My bus was coming. We rushed in opposite directions through the door and collided head-on.

"Excuse me!" Sun Li exclaimed, clearly distressed at having run headlong into a foreigner.

"No, it's my fault," I said.

"May I help you with your bags?" Sun Li asked in surprisingly correct English.

"No," I replied, "they're very heavy. I can take them. But what is your name?"

Sun Li suddenly grew self-conscious. Her eyes fixed on the floor, she giggled shyly behind her hand and said, "My name is Sun Li, and I work in the ticketing office."

"Do you?"

"Yes, if you ever need any help, I would be glad to assist you."

"Thank you, I'll remember that."

"Excuse my bad English," Sun Li added quickly. "I am only a student and I have never talked to a foreigner before."

"Your English is perfect," I assured her as I picked up my bags and began to run towards the bus.

"Goodbye." Sun Li waved and smiled. "Remember me!"

I flew to Beijing on a forty-seat propeller plane. The American who sat beside me, a lawyer working for an international firm with a branch in Beijing, spoke Mandarin fluently. He had travelled to Hefei to investigate the case of a peanut butter factory. The machinery, the company had claimed, was defective and had brought about the bankruptcy of the factory. My American friend had gone into the factory with a video camera in search of evidence. It looked to him as if someone had purposely damaged the machines in order to collect the insurance. He videotaped as much as he could. The managers tried to stop him. Now, with the thundering of the propellers and the thought of the peanut butter, he wavered, nauseated. As for me, I felt light-headed: it was my first spring in China.

In Beijing, the willow and poplar trees lining the road from the airport waved their graceful green branches in the wind. It was the season for admiring flowers in Yuanming-yuan Gardens, the Garden of Perfect Brightness; for trailing willow branches behind a slow boat as you rowed to the mid-dle of the lake beside the Summer Palace; for gathering blos-soms in the orchards outside the city. All weekend long, I had been filled up with good things: Peking Opera and mutton kebabs, dragon kites flying high on May Day in Tiananmen, and the other-worldliness of the Summer Palace. Far off in the distance, the Fragrant Hills were astir with new green. At the end of the weekend, the dean called me to say the con-tract would be mailed to me and he'd look forward to seeing me when classes began in September.

When I arrived back in Hefei on Monday morning, there was a note waiting for me at the guest-house. It was from Sun Li and it read, "Please come to visit me in my room at the Air China office sometime." I arranged to go the next Sunday.

Adjacent to the ticketing office, Sun Li's room had the look of an office hastily converted into a dormitory. Two narrow cots, one of them vacant, huddled against opposite walls, dwarfed by two huge, office-style windows with no cur-tains on them, which looked out onto the parking lot. At the foot of the bed stood a small metal clothes-closet, the kind used in offices for hanging coats. A dainty little sink with two tiny faucets jutted out of the otherwise barren white wall like some incongruous *objet d'art*. The small clos-et overwhelmed Sun Li's meagre wardrobe: two changes of underwear, two blouses, a skirt, and a dress. On the sink ledge sat only a bar of soap, a toothbrush, and a tube of toothpaste. Sun Li wore no makeup. The room, with Sun Li sitting on one of the small cots, spoke of absolute austerity. It reminded me of a nun's cell, or of a prison cell with barred windows looking out grandly onto nothing at all.

Sun Li smiled at me and asked, "Would you like some tea?"

As we sat and sipped Sun Li's holy mountain brew, we talked. Sun Li came from the north, Liaoning Province, she told me. Her mother worked for the Judicial Bureau in her home town and she had no brothers or sisters. She was studying to be a Air China ticketing agent in Shanghai and had been sent to Hefei for two months to get some on-the-job training.

"What about you, Ha Qisen?" Sun Li asked, using the name she had heard my students and colleagues on campus call me.

I told Sun Li about myself, mostly about the months I had spent in China and the successive phases of my culture shock.

"Ha Qisen," Sun Li pronounced after listening to me for a few minutes, "you are only one-tenth Chinese. You must learn more. Follow me. Do as I do. Be as I am. And you will be all right."

Sun Li's Chinese lessons had to do not only with the Chinese language; they had to do with Chinese life. If someone invited me for dinner, for example, I wasn't to accept until I knew what they wanted from me. In China, Sun Li explained, alluding to what I later identified as the Confucian system of reciprocity, a dinner at the home of friends or acquaintances would immediately put you in their debt.

The lessons went along fine until one spring night when I went to visit Sun Li's dormitory. I knocked on the door. No answer. I went around to the back. A dim light shone through the great office windows. Sun Li was in, but she couldn't hear my knock. I found a small pebble in the parking lot and threw it at the window. It barely made a sound. I found a larger stone. I threw it at the window. This time it went *crash*, right through the glass.

"Who's there?" a man's voice called out in Chinese.

Downtown, within earshot, the students were demonstrating. It suddenly occurred to me that I might be mistaken for a rioter, and if Sun Li answered, she might get into trouble. I panicked. "Wo bu zhidao!" (I don't know!), I cried, then hopped on my bicycle and sped away.

The next morning Sun Li came to my door. "Ha Qisen," she said, "I am glad you have learned something. You did the right thing—to run away. It would be too difficult to explain and it would arouse suspicion. You would lose respect and I would be in trouble. Now let us go and pay for the window quietly. But before we go, I'd like to give you some good news: you are now one-fifth Chinese!"

During the two months she was in Hefei, Sun Li and I spent every Sunday together. We visited a People's Commune, had tea and cake in the Chenghuang Temple Market Teahouse, strolled in Xiaoyaojin Park, ate noodles and *baozi* at the local stands, and drank countless cups of tea in my room. Wherever we went, we practised my lessons in language and in life.

On May 20, Sun Li was scheduled to fly to Shanghai. Though she had worked for Air China for two years, Sun Li had never been on a plane. A week before her departure I received a call from friends in Shanghai who wanted me to meet them on the same weekend. "But would you be able to get a ticket?" they asked. I repeated the question to Sun Li, who smiled at me and nodded serenely.

The afternoon of May 20, Sun Li and I sat side by side as the Shanghai-bound plane waited on the tarmac for the takeoff signal. Sun Li looked at me with a mixture of fear and excitement, and then laughed and reached for my hand. Suddenly, we were speeding down the runway and it was as if it were my own first flight. The moment of takeoff was exhilarating. I felt light as air in the cumbersome propeller jet. The fields of Anhui stretched beneath us and we were circling above them, in a dizzying dance, as the plane turned its nose towards Shanghai.

I remembered a young Chinese student I sat beside on a plane trip from Beijing to Toronto who had been so distraught on takeoff that she lost control of her bladder. But

Sun Li soared, along with the jet. Both of us laughed as we looked out the window at the sun shining through a thick froth of clouds. When we had finished our ascent, Sun Li insisted on giving a further test of my Chinese-ness. For example, could I explain the difference between the words *guanxi* (connections) and *youyi* (friendship)? But I resisted, urging Sun Li to enjoy the view.

Only forty-five minutes away, Shanghai came too soon. The plane touched down, and we scrambled for our bags and disembarked. Outside the airport, Sun Li and I spotted our separate buses. As mine, a downtown bus, pulled up to the stop, I said to Sun Li, "I'd like to see you again before I return to Hefei. Could you come for lunch on Thursday?"

"I'll come to your hotel at eleven o'clock," she replied.

At noon on Thursday, Sun Li and I were eating a meal of special Shanghai noodles and dumplings in the upper-floor restaurant of the Peace Hotel. From the window, we could see the students surging through the street, shouting slogans of protest. But high above the city streets, we felt removed from politics, cloistered temporarily in the peaceful world of our friendship.

After lunch, we shopped at the Friendship Store. I bought Sun Li a pearl necklace with some matching earrings. She bought some "week" rings, a package of seven cloisonné rings each differently coloured, and kept three for herself, giving the other four to me. We promised to trade the rings the next time we met.

In the evening, we took a taxi to a friend's home on Yan'an Lu. A visiting Chinese scholar I had met in Canada, Heping had returned to Shanghai two years before, and I had not seen him since my last trip to Shanghai in November. He had invited me for tea that evening. Sun Li came to help me find my way.

But no one was home, or so it seemed. All the apartments in the cruelly defaced French colonial mansion were locked up tight. No lights shone from the windows, though it was barely nine o'clock. I knocked softly at first, then louder. I called for Heping, hoping he might hear me and come down and open the door. Later, Sun Li wrote to me explaining that Heping had probably not answered the door because of the political situation, that he may have been afraid of being seen with a foreigner.

It was getting late, and Sun Li and I had to go our separate ways across the vast, dark city. I hailed a cab and handed Sun Li the bunch of irises I had bought for Heping. As the cab pulled away, I snapped a photo of Sun Li. She had never looked more radiant than on that night as she stood in the dark street in front of Heping's house, her arms filled with white and coral irises. The pink in the cotton Madras suit I had given to Sun Li echoed the faint glow of roses in her cheeks.

Before we parted, Sun Li and I made plans to meet once more before I left China—when I passed through Shanghai on my way back to Canada. But after the events of June 4, the Foreign Affairs Office at my university booked me on the first available direct flight to Hong Kong. As soon as I arrived back in Canada, I wrote Sun Li to tell her why I had not come to Shanghai to see her.

Soon afterwards, I received this reply:

My dear elder sister Ha Qisen:

I am very pleased to receive the letter from you. Your warm, true, beautiful words made me missing you more deeply. I have been wondering if I have the chance to meet you again and have a wonderful reunion. If not, I think myself as one of the luckiest in the world, for I have a friend, a dearest sister like you. It's ashamed of me that I can't express my feelings in English exactly.

I have learned so much about friendship from you and other people, and found it is so difficult to get real friendship. Most of people would like to be friends when they stay together. But feelings will change easily after they have parted from each other. This is the usual thing. We are not, the feeling between us can never be changed. . . .

I know you are very busy, for you always work and study hard. You keep learning Chinese. I believe you must have made great progress. I will decide if you are 25% or 50% Chinese after I have given you a test. You escaped from the test I wanted to give you on the airplane on our way to Shanghai. It's the first thing to examine you when we meet again.

Dear elder sister, I hope you are happy lucky forever. Please give my warm regards to your parents.

your younger sister,
Sun Li

Now whenever I plan to visit China, I write to Sun Li. We have arranged to meet in Beijing, in Shanghai, then in Guangzhou. We even planned for me to visit Shenyang, where she now lives. But the plans never worked out. Once, I was called away for unexpected meetings. Another time, Sun Li was unable to get holidays; and another, she couldn't reach me to arrange a time and place to meet. The places I stayed in China rarely had telephones. Or if they did, I didn't know the numbers in advance. And it was just as difficult for me to reach Sun Li. Like so many private residences in China, her mother's home had no telephone, and whenever I tried to contact Sun Li at the Air China office, my call was lost in a sea of bureaucracy.

Still, Sun Li and I write from time to time, and we promise not to forget each other. Some spring soon I know we will meet again. But sometimes I wonder if Sun Li will be disappointed when she sees me again. Will it seem to her that I have lost all my Chinese-ness? Or, once I see her, will the Mandarin come streaming forth, like some fountain of living waters, and Sun Li be assured that we are still and always will be much more to each other than *guanxi*?

A Trip to Bountiful Harvest

FUYANG CITY DRAWS its name from the most poetic and practical of conceptions. *Fu*, my students told me, means "rich and bountiful harvest," and *yang* means sunshine. A fully northern town, Fuyang is the equivalent of Ontario's North Bay or even Gravenhurst, where Norman Bethune himself grew up and where many Canadians pass the idyllic summers of their childhood. Babies arrayed in colourful quilted bunting bags, men wearing hats lined with rabbit fur, and shops packed tight with the most inexpensive of bulky down jackets also make you think of Siberia, even though, in November, no snow, only soot-laden winds, gust through the streets of the city. But the cuisine in Fuyang draws your thoughts westward, along the silk road, to the Middle East. Muslim restaurants serve up the most delectable of dishes: flat breads, kebabs, and other Middle Eastern specialties that you would never expect to find in this part of China.

No scholar had visited Fuyang City—famous for its rabbit fur, its leather, its dust, and its Old Well Wine—since before Liberation in 1949. And no one knew when another scholar would come. From what I gathered, my visit was an important occasion for the city, and especially for the teachers' college that had invited me. I found out later that the teachers had conferred for hours about what to feed me and where to house me. Apparently the municipal Party officials had gone to as much trouble. The first night a great banquet, presided over by the Party secretary, was laid out in my honour. At the banquet, toasts were made to me and to my country, its virtues and its heroes.

"When I think of Canada," the Party secretary said, "I think of Norman Bethune."

"When I think of Canada," the second-in-command of the ceremonies whispered dreamily, "I think of wheat, fields and fields of wheat." He paused. "And of Norman Bethune!"

"And when I imagine Canada," said the last official who ranked high enough to merit an opinion, "I think of trees—trees and trees and trees. And of snow. So much snow . . ."

I pulled my jacket closer. Fuyang was actually far colder than Toronto, where I grew up. And there we had central heating. Still, I smiled as I reminded myself that the last official's vision of Canada was no more fanciful than mine had been of China—of a country memorable chiefly for its ancient pagodas, intricate classical gardens, and expanses of bamboo forests.

I might have felt honoured had I been the invited guest, but the truth was I was an impostor. I had taken the place of Dan, a fellow teacher at our university and professor of religion from Seattle, who had, the week before, come down with a cold and was too weak to make the long car journey north in the cold weather. It was his knowledge of abstruse metaphysical subjects the Chinese teachers wanted. But here I was instead, an English teacher with only a smattering of poems in hand and some hastily put together lectures.

The morning after the sumptuous official banquet to welcome me, I was taken to the college to meet some of the teachers. At first reticent, they soon began to speak eagerly of the new ideas that had been flooding into Fuyang since the city had opened up to the world in 1984. Freud had just been translated into Chinese, one teacher in her forties told me excitedly. She was reading his work on dreams and writing an article applying some of his theories to one of Zhang Yimou's films, *Hong Gaoliang (Red Sorghum)*.

That night I showed slides of my travels in India to the students of the college. As soon as the last slide had flickered off, a small band of girl students rushed to the front of the room to give me bouquets of roses. I could not imagine where they would find roses in Fuyang in November. As they presented their small bouquets, they hugged me and cried openly, pleading for a closing song. An evening with students in China, I found, often ended with everyone raising his or her voice to the night as if to place a seal, like a kiss, on the precious hours of intimacy shared. Likewise, this evening ended with the students, all five hundred of them, singing "Tonight Must Not Be Forgotten" as well as the three Canadian songs I had taught them: the Native "Land of the Silver Birch," the French "Vive Les Canadiennes," and the British "The Maple Leaf Forever."

After we finished singing, the students escorted me to the Dean's Office, where I was presented with several beautiful gifts, including a lovely selection of Chinese paper-cuttings, a specialty of Fuyang, and a book about the city entitled *Fuyang—Open for Business*. The paper-cuttings depicted traditional themes. One was an intricately patterned rendering of the characters for "Double Happiness," characters symbolizing love and marriage. Entitled *Back to Parents' Home*, another showed a young peasant man leading his bride on a donkey piled high with gifts of household items, her dowry.

The final two gifts were exquisite beyond imagining: a Chinese brushstroke painting by a local artist of a rose, the symbol of Fuyang, at the very moment of its unfolding, and a piece of poetry inscribed in calligraphy. Later on, when I asked some students and colleagues in Hefei if they'd like to try their hand at translating the poem, I was offered two different versions. The first was by the dean of my department, an urbane and sophisticated Shanghainese, and it read,

"In Praise of You"

You are like an angel
with all the qualities of an angel,
physical beauty as well as inner virtue.
You are an angel in the mist,
giving radiance and kindness
to all around you.
You are an angel dancing in a grotto.

A second translation by one of my students was probably less accurate, but I preferred its simplicity:

The beautiful girl danced towards the wind
like a fairy girl,
the smoke and the fog just curling over the flowers.
Look at so many grottos!
In nearly everyone,
you can find a fairy girl.

At the end of the gift-giving session, the dean and vice-dean of the college posed for an official photo with me. Then the student leaders whisked me away to a dance party taking place in one of the classrooms. From that evening, I have two pictures side by side in my photo album: one of myself with the dean and vice-dean holding up two pieces of rice paper, one adorned with calligraphy and the other with the slowly opening rose; and an unofficial photo of myself with watering eyes, holding a small bouquet of red roses and embracing a young girl student named Double Mei as another girl student looked on shyly.

When I arrived back in Hefei, I shed my People's Liberation Army coat. It was warmer down south, and I didn't need it anymore. The other foreign teachers laughed heartily when I told them about the banquet put on for me and the comparison implied between me and Norman Bethune. As I put away the last of the photos, I couldn't help feeling a twinge of embarrassment. I hadn't even been the expected guest, yet Fuyang had opened up its arms to me.

I wondered if Norman Bethune had felt the same inexplicable gratitude not only for the predictable kindness of the Chinese people but for the way they loved you so indiscriminately, despite your human flaws. I remembered the openness of Double Mei's face as she and her five roommates served me fresh sesame cakes and tea one afternoon in their dormitory. As a gift to honour my visit, they had presented me with a three-volume set of the classic Chinese novel *A Dream of Red Mansions*, which I could not read, and a small card in English, which I could. On the back of an old Valentine's card, Double Mei had scrawled these words: "Fare you well, fare lady. Meeting you was the rage of the day!"

Dancing at the Dongpu Reservoir

I BEGAN, AS I WOULD any introductory English course, with Chaucer. The students' favourite pilgrim on the journey to Canterbury was Madame Eglantyne. When I asked Miss Zhu what "eglantyne" meant, she whispered her answer.

"Wide nose?" I asked, certain that I had misunderstood her.

She spoke louder. I still couldn't hear her. She spoke louder still, her voice ascending from a whisper to a stage whisper. "Wild rose!" she exclaimed.

As far as I knew, no wild roses grew in Hefei, so I wondered how Miss Zhu would know the name of this species of flower. My suspicions were confirmed when, at the end of the class, one of the students told me that Miss Zhu had read from a footnote in the text written in Chinese characters, which I could not understand.

I had been in China only two weeks when Teachers' Day arrived—September 10. At the end of my lecture on "Popular Ballads," the section following Chaucer in our textbook, the class monitor presented me with a local handicraft: a simple, blue-framed piece of artwork made from shells arranged in the shape of a bird and entitled *Beautiful Jade.*

I was enchanted. The way the students were treating me could not be compared to anything I had experienced as a teacher in Canada. But it was not only the gift on Teachers' Day that impressed me (how remarkable even, I thought, that such a day should be celebrated!). Still imbued with the Confucian ethic of respect for the teacher, the students frequently surprised me with their thoughtfulness.

Each morning the class rose as I walked into the room and said, "Good morning, Teacher!" The class monitor then wiped the chalk dust from the chair in front of my desk and from the podium, with its red star on the front. At break time, one of the students rushed to the teachers' lounge to fill my lidded cup with *kaishui* (boiling water). At the end of the class, the same student who had wiped clean the chair and podium stayed behind to erase any markings I had made on the blackboard. Meanwhile, another student came forward to carry my books.

I asked Mr. Qian, the volunteer that day, "But why should you carry my books?"

"Because I am a boy and you are my teacher," he replied.

"But they're heavy!"

"Not for me! For boys, books like these are as light as a feather."

In the third and final year of their university studies, the students in my "Grade Three" class, as they called their year, were an odd mixture of innocence and sophistication, of ingenuousness and polished elegance. Though most were in their early twenties, they still referred to themselves and to each other as "girls" and "boys." But when addressing one another in class or before the teacher, they always used the formal "Miss" or "Mr." before the surname. And occasionally, one of the more courteous boy students would even bow slightly before presenting his opinion to the teacher and the class.

Though only the most exceptional students would ever be assigned to teach English at a university, all seemed sincerely interested in literature, even in Chaucer, and I was surprised when they responded with genuine delight to "Robin Hood and Allin-a-Dale," a ballad about thwarted love, arranged marriage, and a happy change of fortune in which the lovers of the poem are united at last. The poem seemed to have a relevance for them I could not imagine it having for Western students. It was difficult not to be impressed.

I assigned seminars to each student and set the topic for the first essay, due two weeks later; they were to analyze the excerpts in our textbook from *The Merchant of Venice, Twelfth Night,* or *Hamlet.* I waited, eager to hear the first seminar and receive the essays. Hong Tian (Red Sky) was up for the first seminar, on Shakespeare's sonnet "Shall I compare thee to a summer's day?"

Like most of my girl students, Hong Tian had a deskmate with whom she walked around the campus holding hands, a sign of close friendship between young women in China. Hong Yu (Red Rain) was also Hong Tian's roommate, one of the seven girls assigned to share her dormitory room. The two Hongs ate rice together in the cafeteria, walked to classes together, and studied in the library together in the evenings.

Both Hong Tian and Hong Yu were renowned on campus for their beauty, and wherever they went, they attracted stares and inspired furtively whispered comments. Actually, Hong Tian was the great beauty of the school, but somehow, in the same way the moon basks in the reflected glory of the sun and receives its light from it, Hong Yu had acquired something of Hong Tian's radiance.

On the day of her seminar, Hong Tian was absent from class. I wondered what had happened to her, and so I asked Hong Yu. She answered, "It is impossible to say."

"Is Miss Hong ill?" I asked.

"Perhaps," replied Hong Yu.

Clearly Hong Yu did not wish to reveal the reason for Hong Tian's absence. I went ahead with the class on Shakespeare's sonnets, collecting the first essays at the end of my three-hour lecture.

That night I began to read the students' papers. I started with Hong Tian's commentary on Malvolio, handed to me by Hong Yu. It read as follows:

> The aim of comedy is to reflect in a humorous way, human limitations. He [Malvolio] was laughed at by the audience in many respects—being arrogant, being in a one-sided love state, being pompous, being blind in knowing the true nature of the surrounding circumstances, being jealous, being stupid in realizing what is beautiful and what is awkward and ugly, being stubborn, as well as being too simple of mind. . . .

The analysis was passable. I read on to the end. Hong Tian did not falter. I gave her a *C.*

I went on to Hong Yu's paper, also on Malvolio. I began reading:

> The aim of comedy is to reflect in a humorous way, human limitations. He [Malvolio] was laughed at by the audience in many respects—being arrogant, being in a one-sided love state, being pompous, being blind in knowing the true nature of the surrounding circumstances, being jealous, being stupid in realizing what is beautiful and what is awkward and ugly, being stubborn, as well as being too simple of mind. . . .

Was I seeing things? It was late. Perhaps I was reading Hong Tian's paper again? I turned to the back to check the signature. The paper was signed "Hong Yu."

The next day I had no classes. I went to visit Hong Tian, hoping I would also find Hong Yu in the dormitory.

We all needed to talk. I knocked on the door. Someone invited me to come in. I opened the door. Hong Tian lay on her cot, facing the wall. I called out her name. She turned over and looked at me in surprise, her eyes red from crying.

It wasn't that she had anything personal against her classmate Miss Zhu, Hong Tian explained, but just that she wanted her brother, a local factory worker who was established in the city now, to help her stay in the city. Hong dreaded returning to her small town in the countryside. But recently, her brother had fallen in love with Miss Zhu and was now devoting his energies to helping her instead. Tensions had risen between the two classmates, and Hong and Zhu had descended to blows. Distraught, Hong Tian had been crying for two days. As for the Shakespeare essay, what could she do under the circumstances but ask Hong Yu to help her?

I decided to give Hong Tian and Hong Yu passing grades. I put the incident from my mind and went on with the class. *Paradise Lost* was our next work. I assigned the seminar introducing the poem to Miss Zhu. On the day of her seminar, Miss Zhu's place was empty. I asked if there were any questions about the poem, hoping that by the end of these questions Miss Zhu would arrive.

"Tell us more about the Garden of Eden," Miss Pang said.

I read the students the relevant passages from Genesis and explained briefly the biblical story of the fall.

Miss Pang asked, "Do you believe in original sin?"

Where was she picking up such morsels of Christian theology, I wondered. I offered a metaphorical reading of the fall as a symbolic story: Eve was emotion; Adam was reason; and the serpent, symbolizing humanity's lower nature, was what took over when reason and emotion were at odds with one another.

Fifteen minutes passed. Miss Zhu was still absent. Her deskmate's place was also empty. Then Miss Cheng arrived, breathless with the news, "Miss Zhu has a high fever. She will not be able to come to class today!"

Another time, two girl students, deskmates who were both named Xu (pronounced *shoe*), left a note under my door the night before their joint seminar was scheduled to be presented. It read:

Dear Dr.,

We implore your forgiveness for our failing grades and ask that you grant us some reprieve from the seminar. We are so worried, we cannot concentrate on our studies and surely will be devastated by any failure.

more sincerely,
your two Xus

Almost every time a girl student and half of the times a boy student was up for a seminar presentation in class, some calamity would befall him or her. I took Hong Tian aside and asked for an explanation.

"You see, in China," she explained, "the students, especially the girls, do not like to speak in class. Out of respect, everyone prefers to listen to the teacher."

Miss Hong's explanation was confirmed by the way Mr. Chen prefaced his seminar on Milton the next week. In the tradition of Chinese self-effacement and modesty, Mr. Chen asked us, his listeners, to forgive him for presenting his "poor opinion of *Paradise Lost.*"

I had had enough. The next day I cancelled all seminar presentations and added an additional written assignment to the course. The next work on the syllabus was *Pilgrim's Progress.* I had no idea whether a work like this, a religious allegory, would make any sense to students who had received their primary-school education at the height of the Cultural Revolution. As Cao Meihua explained to me, education then had consisted of shouting slogans and crossing out the names in the history texts of those figures no longer in favour.

"What is the significance of this work for us today?" I asked the class.

Hong Tian answered, "It teaches us to tolerate people of other religions. In Chinese, we have a saying: 'That which is different is golden.'"

I was mystified. Such liberal, open-minded interpretations of texts co-existed with the most unforgiving attacks of Marxist literary criticism. For example, Milton was "the greatest poet of the bourgeois revolution of the mid-seventeenth century," and Alexander Pope a satirist who wrote during "the reactionary regime of the Restoration."

Most orthodox of all was Miss Pang's interpretation of *Robinson Crusoe*, taken in full from Marx. Robinson Crusoe, I learned from reading Miss Pang's essay, was a man who derived the satisfaction of seeing the fruits of his own labour. That was good, she conceded, but the principle needed to be extended from the individual to the whole society.

After I had picked up my monthly salary of fifteen hundred *yuan*—a salary several times more than what the Chinese teachers made, with an additional fifty *yuan* thrown in for my "pork allowance"—I seriously considered leaving China. In their characteristically intuitive way, my students sensed my discouragement. They sent a delegation to my room to invite me to sing a song of my choice at an English salon. The note read, "Humbly request your presence for English Party at the White House"—the students' name for the building housing the seat of power, the Foreign Affairs Office.

A few minutes later, Mr. Chen, the class monitor, came to tell me, probably out of pity for my fruitless efforts, that he was "a better person" for my classes on English literature. Miss Pang, probably from the same motivation, came a few minutes later to tell me I had "a holy mind." With her was Miss Tang, who added her vote of confidence in my abilities as a teacher: "We Chinese students are afraid of English poetry. We are told that it is beautiful but very difficult to understand. You have shown us the beauty. This is the first step."

After they had all left, Wu Hong burst into my room determined to disabuse me of any lingering idealism I might have about the potential of my Grade Three students. "Forget about them! They come from the countryside. They're not interested in education; they just want to find a way to stay in the city. Concentrate on what's most important: your writing about China!"

I told Wu Hong I had no plans to write about China, except perhaps for the occasional article for a newspaper back home. But Wu Hong knew I was keeping a diary. She had often made suggestions for the day's entries. I supposed she was referring to it.

The Spring Festival vacation arrived. One of my girl students gave me a card with a blonde woman and a blond man on the front. An arrow pointing to the blonde woman was followed by my name. Inside, she had scribbled these words:

> A nice greeting, representing a girl's care, a girl's heart.
> Let your wish, your happiness be fulfilled at the moment
> of opening this card slightly. . . .

Attached was a small gift typical of the kind of kitsch that helps keep China's economy booming—a round piece of plastic with a cat painted on both sides. A little tag was taped to it and it read:

> This late-coming gift brings you Extra-Happiness. The
> two-sided cat wishes you Double-Happiness.

Double Happiness—"double" because anything single in China is felt to be part of a sad and lonely affair. It is significant that the Chinese character for *hao* (good) is composed of the characters for woman and for man placed side by side. I wondered if my students would surprise me by

147

arranging a marriage for me in time for the Chinese New Year. For them, an engagement to be married was an achievement to be flaunted far more than was an *A* from me.

The Spring Festival vacation came and went. No marriage was arranged and no engagements announced. On the last Monday of February, my Grade Three students reassembled in my classroom ready to attack Shelley's "Ode to the West Wind." It was obvious to them: the "Pestilence-stricken multitudes" were the peasants of Paris, the proletariat, and the West Wind was the coming revolution that would sweep aside the reign of tyranny by the oppressors— read "capitalists"—and bring about a socialist society, or "spring."

We went on to the moderns. "Yeats' 'No Second Troy,' " Hong Tian ventured, was "like sunlight on our shoulders." I set one of the sonnets from W. H. Auden's sonnet sequence "In Time of War" as a sight poem for the class, just to see if anyone had learned anything about how to read poetry: "But in the evening the oppression lifted; / The peaks came into focus; it had rained. . . ."

I don't think the students had a clue what the poem was about. The essays they wrote were desperate fabrications. But it didn't matter. I had given up my mission of teaching Chinese students English literature some weeks before. What good would it do them anyway? The more I learned about the lives they were destined to live, the more I understood their disinterest in literature.

Assigned to live in places not of their choice, to do work also not of their choice and for which they were often not suited, and sometimes even obliged to marry someone they did not love just to fulfil a social obligation at the appropriate time in life and to have a partner with whom to brave the stormy monotony of their prearranged lives, my students took little pleasure in the world of the imagination. Most were far too disconsolate for that, and they had never learned to use literature as Shelley had in his ode—to imagine change.

One day I looked out to find that the tips of the *ba-jiao* leaves on either side of the grove met in the middle, forming a shady bower. I cycled to class now without even a sweater and often passed by Hong Tian and Hong Yu walking along the paths of the university with parasols—really umbrellas—as they held hands and hummed "Auld Lang Syne." Like most young city women in China, they anxiously guarded the whiteness of their skins.

That afternoon I went to get my mail in the teachers' lounge. I opened the one envelope waiting for me there and found this note:

> Dear Dr.,
> We understand that you will returning to your homeland soon, so we would like to invite you to a picnic with your Grade Three class. We are sure to go tomorrow. We will start at 7:30 a.m. from the cement playground beside building 207 and 208. Do please arrive on time.
>
> > Yours,
> > Miss Pang

The next day was a warm Saturday in April. We set off on our bicycles, travelling west of the city. Within minutes, we were in the countryside. Only a few rustic peasant dwellings and the occasional commercial enterprise dotted a sea of rippling green. To the left stood a bicycle factory and a building-materials shop with bamboo poles stacked high against the front of the shop door; and to the right, a food vendor sat in his stall selling "orange juice," a kind of sickly sweet pop, and rolls made from the whitest, most glutinous of breads to the students who stopped to buy a picnic lunch for the class.

We turned right down a narrow country road, exhaling as we did the last vestiges of city smog. On either side of the road for several miles, poplar trees rustled in the April wind. In the fields to the left and to the right, a great blaze of winter jasmine flared as far as the eye could see. Because

149

of the shortage of bicycles (and also because most of my girl students did not ride bicycles—too dangerous, they said), Hong Tian rode on my rear carrier. Though she was very petite and not very heavy, she continually expressed amazement at my ability to endure the load. As soon as the Dongpu Reservoir came into view, she asked me to stop and take a photograph of her and several other girls sitting in the field of winter jasmine.

All around us the golden winter jasmine shone, illuminating the field with its small globes of light. The fresh spring air, the splendour of the fields, the green surrounding us—all seemed to give new life to my students. With each mile that separated them from the city, they became increasingly changed: their eyes brightened; they lost their shy reserve with one another and began laughing and joking; and with a huge burst of energy, the boy students vied with one another to see how light they could make their load of girl students seem.

We arrived, at last, at the Dongpu Reservoir. We chose a spot beside a cool, crystalline stream, with swiftly flowing aqua waters and a wealth of colourful shells and pebbles sparkling on its bed. In an unusual act of abandon, some of the girl students took off their shoes, rolled up their slacks, and began to wade in the water, bending over from time to time to peer at the riverbed and choose a pebble or shell that caught their eye. Other students found a grassy knoll surrounded by trees and set down some blankets and a Sony Walkman, brought for the purpose, I supposed, of blasting Chinese rock music into the quiet world of the reservoir.

Hong Tian seemed more relaxed than I had ever seen her. Her hair was dishevelled, but she was smiling as she set out the bread, the pickled vegetables, the drinks, and the cakes. In a rare moment of reconciliation, Miss Zhu was working right beside her. As they laid out the lunch, Hong and Zhu exchanged thoughts about what should go where. And for once, Mr. Chen, the class monitor, had abandoned the habitual dutifulness that always seemed to oppress him. He was teasing Miss Pang in a delightfully silly and endearing way by pulling her ponytail.

Could these be my students? It was as if an invisible veil had been lifted and they had passed into another world more beautiful even than any portrayed in the works of literature we had studied. And to top things off, the willowy Miss Pang was falling into the embrace of the slight Mr. Chen as he swept her around the grassy knoll in a skilful waltz.

Hong Tian followed with Mr. Bai; Hong Yu with Mr. Li. And the girls and boys who were shy danced with their deskmates. The tapes were blaring—waltzes, tangos, rumbas. The Sony Walkman had been brought not to play the latest rock and roll but music for ballroom dancing. As I sat with Miss Zhu watching and smiling, Mr. Qian, the one who so often insisted on carrying my books, approached me and asked me to dance. I danced. And I danced. And everyone danced with me until it seemed we had left the old world behind and become part of a new order of things in which everyone was a spirit of the grassy knoll, a god or goddess in some Chinese pantheon of nature deities.

The strains of the music began to ebb. Each dancing couple settled onto the blankets that had been laid on the grass. Then Mr. Chen turned the music off. The sudden silence found us tightly bound together in a moment of unexpected intimacy. "I have an announcement to make," he said. "I would like to recite for you a poem I have learned in honour of our teacher. We haven't studied it, but it's by my favourite poet, Tennyson. He began:

> . . . Come, my friends,
> 'Tis not too late to seek a newer world.
> Push off, and sitting well in order smite
> The sounding furrows; for my purpose holds
> To sail beyond the sunset, and the baths
> Of all the western stars until I die. . . .

151

"Classmates, our dear teacher, I am so sorry, that's all I remember, so good night!" Then, bowing, he turned and fell onto the blanket behind him as everyone laughed and clapped.

When I left China, my students gave me many copies of the pictures we took that day in the field of yellow winter jasmine. I even have some of Hong Tian dancing with Mr. Bai on the grassy knoll at the heart of the Dongpu Reservoir where we picnicked. As I look at their faces, I remember that the students from my Grade Three class are not students anymore. Most are married, some even have children, and all have graduated and been assigned to jobs either in their home town or in the city.

Sometimes, even now, I receive letters from them filled with nostalgia and a twinge of regret for rosebuds, or sprigs of winter jasmine, not plucked in their prime, letters such as these:

> Here everybody's life is as common as certain realistic novels. The world of Shakespearean drama withdraws itself into the background, hides from view. What a shame!
>
> Life is not so promising as I look forward to it; it's not so fantastic as when you were here, at least to me. . . .

I, too, have many memories and some regrets. Sometimes I think about the seminars my students refused to give, or the papers they did write—plagiarism and all. I was not surprised that Mr. Chen got a good job assignment as a translator in the Foreign Trade Department, or that Hong Tian, the most beautiful girl in the school, has still not found someone handsome or successful enough to marry. Perhaps my own life is duller—"not so fantastic"— without them, too, and without dancing at the Dongpu Reservoir on a warm Saturday in April.

SAN CHANG:
IN THE COUNTRYSIDE

Of all the rural places I visited, I was most drawn to San Chang, a typical village in the heart of the Chinese countryside. There, my friend Abel, a Dutch engineer, and his daughter, Anna, were building, together with the Chinese, a ceramic tile factory. San Chang was a fairly modern village and a prosperous one too. Many of the inhabitants owned televisions, and at night you could hear the blare of Chinese programming wafting out into the courtyards, where the water buffalo lowed and the wheat lay drying in preparation for threshing. Beyond the village lights, the moon illuminated the narrow footpaths through the rice paddies.

In San Chang I discovered the true essence of Chinese life—village life. And it was to San Chang I dreamed of returning after I left China in June 1989. Altogether, I spent about a month in San Chang. I would sometimes travel out to San Chang in the factory jeep for day visits with Anna and Abel, or I would catch Bus 33, a rickety old green-and-white bus filled with peasants returning from a day at the city's markets, on a Friday night and spend the weekend. Despite the inroads technology was making into the village, the people still lived in a world apart. The family, the community, and work in the fields or in the factories defined their lives. Life was slow. Love was bountiful. Looking with the eyes of a Western outsider, it is perhaps easy to idealize Chinese village life. But I think I could see the flaws: the tightness of the community must have been suffocating for the young people, and the repetitiveness of life—generation after generation living as its parents had—must have been stifling. Now the new technology was bringing change, connecting the villagers to the wider world. People began to dream of going waibian *(outside). Some even began to idealize the life lived beyond the confines of the village. The young people, especially, yearned for broader scope. As one village teenager put it, "I would like to go outside because my world is very small and the outside is very big."*

One night, as I walked along a footpath between two rice paddies, I encountered two elderly women and a child, a grandmother carrying her grandchild as she strolled with her friend. Though their accent was heavy, I was able to converse with them a little. In their own humorous way, they expressed the feeling that was growing in the hearts of so many people in the village: a dislike of being cut off from the outside world. Television had made them feel that way. They were interested in the life of local cities, of other provinces, and even of other countries. Most never would go "outside," but, increasingly, the outside was coming to them in the form of foreigners such as Abel, Anna, and myself.

Like many peasants first experiencing modernization, the villagers did not have a full appreciation of the beauty of their own pattern of life. I think of a night around Christmas when the electricity went off in the village. For a brief interlude, there were no radios or televisions. Life was as it had been of old. People strolled the pathways of the village, children made a game of catching fireflies, and the shape of the moon and the colour of the sky were the main topics of conversation.

Once the opera came to play in the village auditorium, an old Communist meeting place with a red star on its frontispiece. Throughout the performance, the villagers signalled their satisfaction with a throaty "hao" (good). Sometimes at dusk, a farmer would repeat the arias as he drove his water buffalo through the rice paddies. At such times, I became aware how myth and history live in the mind of the Chinese peasant, in a way we from the modernized West can scarcely imagine. For him, stories are in the very soil: it speaks to him of the past, of his ancestors, and of many strange and wonderful events that still cast their mysterious glow on his own ordinary life.

In the end, I came to see San Chang as a place of ingathering, a village in a promised land where people congregated for no particular reason other than that destiny had placed them there. Destiny, perhaps the most powerful of reasons, had brought them home. The villagers were diverse, drawn as they were from a diaspora of Chinese. And then there were we three foreigners: Abel, Anna, and me. Together, we formed a cluster of wayfarers. What could a peasant, half-Russian and half-Chinese, an Indian from the American navy, a Dutch engineer and his daughter, a Canadian teacher, and several hundred Chinese peasants have in common except San Chang? San Chang—a village in the Chinese countryside, remote from politics and the affairs of the world, where human love could sprout up among such vastly different people as to make the stars wink with astonishment.

Waibian

"HERE, I GIVE HIM TO YOU. Take him to the outside." The grandmother with iron-coloured hair pushes her only grandson towards me. She is laughing. He is covered only by a small square of red cloth tied by two thin strings at the back. It is eight o'clock in the morning and already eighty-six degrees. A light breeze blows off the fields. In every direction emerald green rice paddies glisten, catching the sun on their liquid surfaces.

In San Chang, *waibian* (outside) means the city of Hefei, only ten miles away. It means Shanghai or Nanjing. These days it may even mean a foreign country—*waiguo*, where I come from. I am *lao wai*, an "outlander."

From San Chang, it is not easy to go outside. Lao Cheng waited thirty-one years to do so. During the Anti-Rightist Campaign of 1957–58, he was "sent down" from Shanghai to the countryside. Only this past spring, after thirty one years in San Chang, did he return to the city of his birth. The villagers in San Chang held a farewell party

156

for him. His eyes glistened as he left. San Chang had become first a habit and then a home. He walked away from the village carrying nothing.

Old Zhou is still waiting to leave San Chang. Or maybe he has given up trying. When you walk through the market he greets you with "Good morning! American navy." He has put in forty-one years at San Chang. Why did he come? Because the leaders told him to. He was a marine once. He sailed the seas. Now he is too old to go outside, even if he could get an identity card that would allow him to relocate.

Before Liberation in 1949, San Chang was a simple farmers' village like any other and not called San Chang, meaning Third Factory, but Chao Hu Village. Then, in the 1950s, a penal colony was established here. Because the earth around the village is rich in clay, prisoners could be occupied making bricks. The village changed its name and became home to the Third Factory for the Production of Building Materials, created to make work for prisoners: thieves, murderers, dissenters from various political campaigns, and even soldiers from Chiang Kai-shek's army.

Gradually, four other factories grew up in San Chang: a machinery factory, a roof-tile factory, a cement factory, and a second brick factory. Despite the archaic methods of firing kilns, smelting iron, and drying bricks, production plodded on and the factories drew workers from as far away as Huainan. Before long, farmers, too, were working in the factories and farmers' sons and daughters were leaving school to drive tractors loaded with bricks and to haul coal for the kilns. The children of the village grew up in the shadow of the smokestacks.

Today, the village *is* its factories. Peasants, workers, and the original prisoners live together in San Chang. There are eight hundred inhabitants in all. An additional two hundred commute from Hefei to work in the factories by day, returning to the city at night. An Indian lives here and a Russian of mixed race. The Russian is a remnant from the days of Sino-Soviet friendship. Both look thoroughly

Chinese. Both speak only the local dialect. Their mother tongues are a distant memory. They go to market at six o'clock in the morning to buy vegetables with the others, and at night they, too, sit in the community hall smoking or playing mah-jong for clothespegs.

Work here is good. In 1989, factory workers made about forty *yuan* a month. Farmers make almost as much, adding to their income by growing vegetables in private plots and selling them on the free market—an agricultural reform called the "household responsibility system." The Anhui countryside was the first to experiment with the system. Now San Chang prospers because of it.

Businesses spring up everywhere. In one year, a new restaurant and five roadside stands selling cigarettes and soft drinks have appeared. The Lius and the Wangs both have new two-storey homes built from cement and bricks. At night, in a quiet courtyard of the village, the light from a black-and-white television flickers on the hardened earth. Families and neighbours gather around to watch the weather report during planting season. So do the geese and chickens. Just outside the door, the old men doze on bamboo mats under the stars.

The new ceramic tile factory, a Dutch-Chinese joint venture, will revolutionize the life of the village. When it begins production, all the other factories in the village will shut down: they use too many materials for only a small profit. The clay is running out. There is overproduction. These days bricks are piled seven feet high all around the village market. The new factory will have quality control. There will be larger profits. The tiles will be exported to Europe. Then everyone will work with the foreigners.

Mr. Qu owes his job to the new factory. He cooks for the foreigners who live in San Chang and those who pass through to visit the factory. He knows what foreigners like to eat and drink. He knows when they rise in the morning and when they go to sleep. He has a picture-book of Holland with photos of windmills in it. He changes foreign money on the black market and makes a profit. He buys a refrigerator, a ghetto-blaster, and a colour television. He watches the news. He knows that the foreign friends are bringing prosperity to China.

But the children of the village couldn't care less about the foreigners or the new factory. When they are not grazing water buffalo or hauling water for their mothers, they are sitting in the village doorways writing Chinese characters in white chalk on the cement, or devising other, more exotic activities. One child has two pet bats. He has tied them with a long string to the leg of a chair. He likes to watch them spread their wings as they set off in flight around the room.

But the best game of all is picture-taking when the foreigners walk through the village on Sundays. The children pose in a group, shy and smiling, then follow the picture-takers. On these sweltering August days, they do not dream of a world beyond the village. A foreigner is something strange, only an amusement to help pass the long summer's day. They are content with their tiny world.

It is evening now. The children have gone inside for rice and vegetables. The factories have shut down for the night. The workers from Hefei board Bus 33 to return to the city. All is quiet. A young boy straddles a water buffalo as it grazes in the fields. A woman draws water from the local well to clean the dinner vegetables. The old men settle in to smoke in the community hall. The last truck filled with bricks rattles towards the town. It grows dark. The village of San Chang closes in upon itself. Fireflies sparkle over the rice paddies—the only light for miles.

The Fate of San Chang

THE FATE OF SAN CHANG rests in Abel's hands and in those of the powers that be: the Hefei Municipal Government, the local Party secretary, Abel's company in Hong Kong and, most of all, the stars. The stars rule over San Chang with their own inscrutable design. Once a typhoon blew up at four o'clock in the afternoon and took with it five square feet of the factory roof. Then the humidity destroyed the machine designed to regulate the amount of clay poured into the slots for brick production. Still, construction inched forward, and, in spite of everything, Abel came to believe in the future of San Chang and to work for it.

Abel is a Dutch engineer and his new ceramic tile factory will be, when it comes into production, a Dutch-Chinese joint venture, exporting fine traditional ceramic tiles to cities all over Europe. The idea for the factory was born in 1987 when Abel went to a conference of ceramicists in Amsterdam, really an excuse for a farewell party for a master of the trade. There, he and a colleague began to talk about the possibility of building a ceramic tile factory in China. They decided that one of them would base him-self in Hong Kong and manage the company, buying machines from old factories in Holland and shipping them to China, while the other worked on-site in San Chang, building the factory brick by brick. They began the work by forming a brokerage company called IMBAS.

Abel made his first trip to China in September 1987 to survey the site where the factory was to be built. Driving through the Anhui countryside, he felt he had entered a world so ancient and remote that there could be no place for him in it. Peasants hauled their produce into town by mule and cart. Women threshed wheat by hand under the noonday sun. Farmers used a simple wooden plough pulled by a water buffalo to irrigate the rice paddies. Old men squatted beside the dusty road smoking long pipes. Abel hung a Dutch flag on a pole in front of the factory liv-ing quarters and planted tulips in the earth beneath it. A child stole the flag and a water buffao ate the tulips, but it didn't matter: Abel was in San Chang to stay.

When Abel began building the factory, the Party secre-tary from the Hefei Public Works Department came daily to oversee construction. An engineer also came from the city to work with—though sometimes it seemed against—Abel. Once Abel lost his patience with them both and went on strike. For a whole week, he just walked around the vil-lage passing the time. The construction of the kiln was not up to standard: the surface was not smooth enough to pro-duce high-quality tiles. He asked the engineer to do it over. The engineer refused.

In the conference that followed, Abel got so bored he counted the hairs—about ten in all—on the engineer's permanently unshaven chin. Though the Chinese had hired Abel, a master craftsman in ceramics, to come to San Chang to lend his expertise to the building of the factory, the locally appointed Chinese managers of the project and the Party secretary, who reigned over them, would not lis-ten to a word Abel said. Endless consultations were called to wrangle, communist style, over every detail of the work on the fledgling factory. It had been like this from the beginning. Abel would give directions and the locals would listen politely, then do exactly as they pleased.

That night Abel demanded for the fourth time in two days that his telephone be connected to *waibian* (outside). Once again, the operator said she had done it. She had not. Abel had not talked to anyone whose tongue he understood in over a month. He threw the telephone out the window. It landed on top of the hydro-transformer and lay there for months, a reminder of the frustration of Abel's early days in San Chang.

Then one night everything changed. The power went out. Abel's chief assistant came by to tell him it would take some time to start the diesel generator for emergency power supply. As Abel gazed out into the dark, the children of San Chang wandered away from their television sets and congregated beneath his window. At first, Abel didn't notice them; then they broke the stillness of the night with a celestial sound. He wept to hear the village children sweetly singing a traditional Chinese melody as they gathered around a single lit candle. Abel went downstairs and taught them an English song in return. They repeated it word for word. One boy wanted Abel to swing him by his arms. Soon others were vying for their turns. It was only three weeks before Christmas, and Abel was surprised to find that he didn't feel homesick.

That February, his first in San Chang, Abel went without heat or hot water in his rooms for three weeks. He could find no fresh fruit or vegetables in the market. The company sent a young apprentice to learn the art of ceramic tile production from Abel. Only two months later, the apprentice went home sick. Abel went on alone, taking his jeep into town once a week to sit in the local hotel and drink beer with the other foreigners. But now, Abel preferred listening to the Huangmei Opera in San Chang to drinking beer in town. Occasionally, an amateur troupe would perform in the village auditorium, and Abel would be invited as the guest of honour. The old men would spit on the floor and drink warm tea out of glass jars. A Shanghainese from the American navy would translate the arias for Abel in very broken English.

The work progressed. Optimistic at first, Abel thought he could finish the factory quickly and bring it into production within one year. But there were unexpected delays. The woman in charge of quality control played with a child instead of inspecting the clay for stones and pieces of old brick. The workers slept on the job, putting off the work with "mingtian" (tomorrow), or "meiyou wenti" (no problem). Nobody understood the high quality required of products for export.

In his frustration, Abel wrote a letter disclaiming all responsibility for an inferior product. He asked the engineer and the directors to sign it. They called a conference of the Chinese workers. Miss Tang, Abel's translator, read the letter aloud, very slowly, in Chinese. They deliberated for several hours, changed a few words, and signed the letter. Abel had won. A few days later, he began to notice a change in the attitude of his workers. Slowly, they began to realize that international standards were not negotiable. They raised the quality of their work just a little, then just a little more. Production at San Chang inched forward.

By April, everyone in the village knew Abel by name, and the children called him by his Chinese name, Aba, which in an ancient tongue means father. He had even learned some Chinese, especially numbers: one o'clock pick-up, sixty *yuan* for groceries, ten more months until production. Abel's daughter, Anna, came to stay with him in the village and learn Chinese. His wife was due to arrive in July. Then came June Fourth. Abel had fought in a war, but he had never witnessed a government crackdown. When the students donned black armbands to mourn the deaths of their classmates, Abel also wore one. But when a convoy of army trucks stopped Abel on his way into the city, he turned back to San Chang and forgot about the crack-down and watched, instead, the old men playing mah-jong in the community hall.

It was planting time in the village of San Chang. Late into the night, the farmers sang sowing songs from ancient times. All the foreigners had left the city. Was it safe for Abel to stay? Someone from the Dutch Embassy came to check on conditions in the village. He left feeling rested. In the countryside surrounding San Chang, the rice slowly ripened under the burning sun. At night, the fireflies danced over the rice paddies. To escape the heat, the farmers were spending almost three hours at *xiuxi* (nap time). By the beginning of August, the decisions taken at the European Community conference on China made it financially impossible to go on. Abel packed his rubber boots in a big wooden crate, nailed it shut, and locked the door to his lodgings. He knew he would be coming back. It was only a matter of time.

He landed a job in Egypt, a three-month contract to build a brick factory in the Nile delta. Since the clay from the banks of the Nile was becoming depleted, he had to develop sophisticated machinery to refine the desert sands into clay for bricks. During those hot Egyptian nights, Abel watched the new moon lying on its side. He meditated on his unfinished factory and brooded over the fate of San Chang. He yearned for a village in the Chinese countryside and prayed to return.

Mr. Qu, the chef, and Miss Tang, the translator, still wait for Abel. The villagers miss Abel too. They remember how on Saturday afternoons he walked through San Chang calling out the traditional Chinese greeting, *Chi fan le ma?* (Have you eaten?), and wishing them a quiet day of rest. On Sunday, he never forgot to "go amen" with Mrs. Hu— to visit the church in town to thank God for rice and all good things, including the factory.

These days, the monsoons blow through San Chang. If Abel were in San Chang tonight, he would walk through the village in his tall boots, an umbrella in his hand. During the day, he would watch the horizon for approaching clouds. He would argue with the Party secretary and curse the engineer, and each day he would check off on his meticulously penned list the tasks done and the tasks yet to do. Each day he would count afresh the months until production, believing that each new setback will somehow bring progress, knowing that the fate of San Chang is sealed. It is in the stars.

Fire and Clay

THE PATH TO THE WANG HOME led right through the heart of San Chang. In the daytime, it took in the whole lively scene of the village: Abel's Hefei Three Factory as it clanked and rattled towards production; the busy market with its fly-ridden slabs of pork and wizened vegetable vendors; the local clinic served by one middle-aged, smiling, white-coated woman doctor; the auditorium with the red star on the top where the opera played; the village *xuexiao* that rang with the singsong voices of small children reciting their numbers, *yi! er! san!*—until, finally, it wound its way out through the cool, green serenity of the rice paddies into the rural part of the village.

If you walked the path at night, there would be hardly a sound, just the faraway rattle of coal trucks lumbering, lights off, down the potholed highway to Hefei from Huainan in the north. But on a dark night, there was much to see on that path: the windows of the single-workers' dormitory richly coloured, like stained glass, by hand washing hung inside to dry; the old men, their blue Mao caps tilted

166

upwards, playing mah-jong for clothespegs inside the community hall; and in the rural part of the village, the flickering violet light of a family television articulating some strange paradox as it played over a water buffalo sleeping in the courtyard.

The Wangs were mostly farmers; that is to say, they lived most of their lives according to the rhythms of rice planting and harvesting. Only very recently had the Wang family joined the world of the San Chang worker, a world so separate from their farmers' life that it seemed to belong to another country and another time. From the ancient world of rural China, the family had somehow passed into a world strangely reminiscent of nineteenth-century England, a crude hell of industrialization in which people no longer measured their days by sunrise and sunset but moved in time to machines. Awake with the nocturnal creatures, all laboured in a perpetual night of toil.

Mr. Wang had been hired on by Abel as a manager in his burgeoning ceramic tile factory. He was in charge of materials, and his work was of great consequence to the fledgling factory, since the quality of the ceramic tiles depended on the purity of the clay which, in turn, depended on the vigilance of the supervisor of materials. Mr. Wang saw to it that all the stones, pebbles, and other extraneous materials were picked out, by hand, from the clay before it was processed.

Abel became close to the Wang family, in part because of Mr. Wang's importance to the factory; but it was as much for some obscure reasons of the heart that Abel showed a tenderness not of this world for the couple and their two daughters. Abel was not a missionary in the ordinary sense of the term: he never tried to convince anyone of his beliefs. Besides, his theology was so eccentric that it was difficult to attach it to any religion in particular, though he professed the Christian faith.

When I asked him his view on life after death, he answered, in his own unique brand of English gleaned

167

from the King James Bible: "In heaven we shall be angels, and there will be no giving or taking in marriage and no separation more." Once he even sent me a written formulation of his creed, the central points of which were that Christ, an "impossible man" who was "as human as God," had a message which, "as dynamite, brings people to fire." To Abel, Christ was someone who "conjures up risks . . . sacrifice," who gave one "a bone to pick with the idols."

Whatever they may have thought of such views, the Wangs reciprocated Abel's feelings with a tenderness that was equally difficult to define. The family showed it by delivering fresh duck eggs and vegetables to Abel's living quarters at the factory, by inviting him for noodles and holy-mountain tea on a Sunday afternoon when he was bound to be lonely, and by placing his photo with those of the ancestors behind the large sheet of glass positioned above the mantelpiece. Though they did not speak of it, Abel understood that the Wangs were Buddhist. On their mantelpiece stood a small china statue of the Laughing Buddha, and on their wall hung a picture of Guanyin.

Abel first took me to visit the Wangs in late May, rice-planting time. When we set out through the delicate maze of footpaths to the Wang home, we lost our way and ended up in a quiet courtyard of the village where wheat lay drying on the hardened earth in preparation for threshing. A startled water buffalo began lowing as we approached, and an elderly woman appeared at the door of the home and announced, "Wang zhi nali" (The Wangs live over there).

As we walked in the direction the woman had pointed, we found ourselves completely alone, surrounded on all sides only by rice paddies. At the edge of one of them lay a newly built grave. In the Buddhist fashion, the grave was sheltered by a low house-like structure and adorned with paper flowers. The cicadas sang. The new moon shed its timid white light on the freshly planted rice paddies. Suddenly, an irregular constellation of fireflies appeared, flickering on and then as suddenly off, like souls sending out one last desperate flare as they passed from this world, or like the earnest prayers of holy ones registering their effects on the world of matter. We heard voices in the distance. From the sound of it, two elderly women were out on the footpaths too, probably to take in the cool night air. As we came closer, we made out a few words through the heavy buzz of their peasant dialect.

"Rain tonight," one said.

"Good for the planting," said the other.

As we drew closer, we discerned the bent forms of the two elderly women through the haze of darkness.

"San Chang, zai nar?" (San Chang, where is it?), we asked. The women smiled and, nodding, pointed the way to Abel's rooms. Inside the factory living quarters at last, we felt relief. There had been nothing to fear out in the rice paddies, yet we felt safer inside where the TV blared out its liturgy of weather forecasts for the various cities of the province. Abel, who out of boredom had taken to parodying the local weatherman, got up and began dancing around the room to the rhythm of his own incantation, a broken Mandarin as primal and compelling as any African drumbeat. "He-fei, tum ... tum ... Bengbu, te ... dum, Ma'an'shan ... da ... dum," he chanted with increasing abandon.

As Abel danced, the storm prophesied by the peasant woman descended upon San Chang. Abel and I rushed to the window and looked out, grateful that we had lost our way to the Wangs' and been saved from being caught in the heavy downpour.

The next morning the countryside was redolent with clean, fresh air. The rain had cleared away the obscuring mists. Even distant Dashu Shan was visible. In the daylight, we had no trouble finding the Wang home. The eldest Wang daughter sighted us first from her bedroom window as she sat at her desk solving math problems, and sprang to her feet. Mr. and Mrs. Wang soon appeared at the door. Before long, the whole family was waving us a welcome.

They had heard of our mishap the night before and, except for the second daughter, who was working a shift at the brick factory, had all been waiting for us.

"Chi fan le ma?" (Have you eaten?), Mrs. Wang asked as she proceeded to her kitchen without waiting for an answer. Abel and Mr. Wang sat down to talk, in their pantomimed way, about the factory, with the eldest Wang daughter, who had the most meagre vocabulary of English phrases, serving as translator. From their talk I gathered that KKK tiles were the most ill-fated tiles in the history of Chinese ceramics. While Abel talked about the recent problems with the factory, Mr. Wang sat on a stool, legs crossed, back hunched, his eyes fixed on some obscure point on the cement floor. Throughout Abel's impassioned monologue, Mr. Wang smoked cigarette after cigarette, nodded, and uttered the occasional throaty "hao" (good). From his confident demeanour and the reassuring glances he periodically cast in Abel's direction, you might almost have thought that Wang had inherited a knowledge of the ancient art of Chinese ceramics from an ancestor who had passed it down in the blood. Yet Mr. Wang was just a farmer showing sympathy to a stranger from a faraway land of which he could barely conceive, having never been away from the village.

Just as the pace of Abel's lamentations was slowing, Mrs. Wang entered the room with two steaming bowls of noodles and some freshly boiled duck eggs. After everyone had eaten, we settled back in silence on the wooden benches. Both the Wangs and Abel had exhausted themselves trying to communicate in a foreign tongue. Not knowing how to bridge the communication gap without words, Abel and I might have excused ourselves had not the eldest Wang daughter broken into the most melancholy Chinese folk song about a little cloud that had travelled all over the countryside only to discover that the life of the people in its home town was best and most beautiful. The only songs Abel and I knew in common were hymns. First, we sang a rollicking chorus of "Onward Christian Soldiers," and then the sweeter, gentler "Amazing Grace."

We left the Wang home late that night, Abel much consoled by his talk with Mr. Wang and I fired by visions of the tiles that Abel's Hefei Three Factory would soon bring into production. Though I had always listened politely, until now I had not been very interested in the building of the factory or in the process to be used in producing the tiles. Now I wanted to see the pit where the clay for the tiles would be dug and to know how it would be transported to the tile factory. I wanted to tour the kilns and to see where the newly made tiles would be dried and stored.

As Abel had explained to Mr. Wang, his were truly Dutch tiles, the kind often seen in the paintings of the Dutch masters, tiles both durable and beautiful. In the words of the colourful advertisement Abel had shown Mr. Wang, "These traditional tiles, with their high quality, their beautiful colours, and their characteristic surface structure, are tiles for all seasons."

As we walked the path that circled the village, Abel explained more about the production of ceramic tiles, specifically about the tiles to be made in San Chang. He began, "Ceramic tiles are made from clay and produced in different shapes, measures, designs, and colours. They can be fabricated on the soft and stiff mud or through the dry process."

We stopped for a minute to look into the clay pit where mud was being excavated for the brick and tile factories already in operation. Before us stretched a world of unredeemed night, a world in which you could imagine the young peasants of the village quickly losing their ambling gait and their rosy-cheeked innocence as they became part of a vast mechanism of moving men and women who worked by the light of the single, fragile string of bulbs hanging over the conveyor belt used to transport the clay from the miry pit to the waiting trucks.

Instinctively, my mind rejected the scene as repugnant.

I tried to imagine what it must have been like here only a few decades ago. I tried to superimpose on the desolate landscape a vision of a quiet world in which the only sound heard after dusk was the lonely echo of a solitary peasant song yodelled by a farmer ploughing as the night fell.

"The aesthetic appearance is very important," Abel continued. The buzz of his voice resonated just beneath the clank and rattle of the machines, insinuating itself into my secret thoughts. "This can be shaped by hand or by machine," he continued. "After shaping, the tiles are dried, and then, glazed or not, they are fired in the kiln at a very high temperature, from 1200°C to 2200°C. The glaze is like a thin glass layer on the surface of the tile and can be shiny or mat." Abel paused. "In San Chang," he concluded, "we want to make two kinds of tiles. One is split tiles, made by the stiff mud process. These will be used for domestic purposes. The other is soft-moulded tiles, and these will be made for export. The first will be produced in natural colours; the second will be glazed in different old-fashioned colours, or unglazed in dark red. These are the well-known Kerkdriel Tiles."

In an instant, at his voice's gentle prodding, new images formed in my mind. Before me, I saw the first truckload of traditional Dutch tiles, in blue, red, and green, ready for shipment to Shanghai and then to Europe where they would adorn the bathrooms, kitchens, and living rooms of numerous homes, modest and elegant. I even imagined the tiles laid on the cement floor of the Wang dwelling, Mrs. Wang scrubbing them down with a primitive, homemade string mop.

"Fire and clay. There is a magic in their marriage," Abel mused.

We walked on through the dark night to the kilns. From where we stood, only several feet away, we could feel the heat radiating from the large ovens. Inside, bricks and tiles were being fired at temperatures beyond imagining, temperatures that would, as if by magic, transform the basest substances into the most solidly durable or the most beautifully exquisite objects: mud into solid red bricks, and clay into tiles or perhaps even Chinese porcelain.

Next, we passed by the brick-storage yards. The tractors were dropping off loads of bricks to be covered with straw mats. Workers walked up and down the lines of drying bricks, periodically lifting the straw mats in order to air them. We had arrived at the village market, a short walk from Abel's rooms. I had lost all sense of time during our tour of the factories. There seemed to be no beginning to the work and no end; the workers' shifts rolled day and night into one indivisible entity. But from the light that was beginning to break over the rice paddies, I discerned that San Chang and its factories were lumbering their way towards another muted, smoke-streaked dawn.

"Now our walk to the end of the world is ended," Abel announced.

Back in the factory living room, Abel searched his desk drawer for a paper and pen. As I sat drinking my nightcap, a cup of holy-mountain tea, he paced the room and then sat down at his desk and began to write. The next morning, as I sat groggy at the kitchen table watching Mr. Qu, the chef, heat my rice gruel, Abel emerged from the living room. He seemed to have slept in his clothes, or perhaps not at all. His hair and clothes were slightly dishevelled, but he didn't look tired.

"I've written something," he announced.

"What?"

"It's called 'A View on Behalf of the Development of Ceramic Products.' I want it to be translated into Chinese so that Mr. Wang and the others can learn the true art of making Dutch tiles."

Abel handed a small wad of handwritten notes to me, and I began to read.

The difficulties raised during the past time in developing glazes for KKK tiles in Hefei III, brought me the following visions:

173

First of all, never say developing glazes, for the glaze is only part of a ceramic product, as there are also the surface, the body, and the total appearance. We have to develop a ceramic product with an attractive, aesthetic, justificated, marketable appearance.

To achieve such a product one needs a developing team with a good vision of the subject. The ceramic medium has a rich potential. It is so various and adaptable that each culture and generation finds in it a new means of expression. As a medium, it is capable of great beauty of form, colour, and texture, and its expressions are unique not only for variety, but also for form and utility as well.

In this idea the KKK-tiles found their beginning, and on this idea the building up of the Hefei III Factory found its origin. . . .

Curious, Mr. Qu walked across the room to the table, carrying my bowl of gruel. He stood with it still in his hand as he leaned over my shoulder attempting to discern the meaning of the squiggles on the handwritten notes. I continued reading:

. . . To make full use of the medium the ceramicist needs not only skill, imagination, and artistic vision. He also needs to have knowledge of the technical side of the matter.

This technical knowledge has not been easy to come by and many of those seriously engaged in ceramics have learned only through endless experimentation and discouraging failures.

While technical information must not be considered as an end in itself, it is a necessary prerequisite to a free and creative choice of means in ceramics.

There, the discourse ended.

"Is there more?" I asked.

"Yes," Abel replied. "There will be more. I will send it to you when it's finished."

The jeep dropped me off that night at the campus and I soon forgot Abel and his factory. I had stacks of papers to mark and lectures to prepare. I became absorbed, once again, in the world of a foreign teacher with students eager to learn about Shakespeare, Thomas Hardy, Margaret Laurence, and other authors. Only a few weeks later, I had to abandon my work as a teacher, because it was feared that China was on the verge of a civil war. Before I left for Canada, I took one last trip to San Chang to store, temporarily, some of my valuables in Abel's rooms—a cloisonné swan, a miniature Chinese screen, some Chinese paintings and calligraphy, a brilliantly coloured silk tapestry made in Xinjiang, and other precious relics of my year in China—until I returned, as I thought I would, the following September.

I didn't return to teach in China that September, and I never did see the rice harvest at San Chang. But Abel wrote to tell me the farmers had had a good year and that the work on the factory progressed steadily, though he regretted he would soon have to return to Holland because his company in Hong Kong was on the verge of bankruptcy. From Holland, he wrote me frequent, passionate letters describing his wishes and his plans for the factory. He also gave me news of the Wang family—the "farmers," as he called them—gleaned from barely decipherable letters that had climbed their way over the many great walls of China, from San Chang all the way to Holland.

With the experience gained from work in Abel's factory, Mr. Wang wrote Abel, he had landed a position as director in one of the local brick factories. His wife still worked as a farmer. The eldest daughter had almost finished high school. The second daughter continued to work nights at the brick factory. Enclosed with the letter was a small note penned by the eldest Wang daughter. In the middle of a red heart she had inscribed the words, "Never forget me."

The following winter I received a letter from Tanta, Egypt. The stationery bore the name of an Egyptian company called Blue Light. Abel's work there, he explained, was to transform the sand of the desert into clay for bricks. Of his life in Egypt, he wrote: "See how the Muslims and Christians live together peacefully here. The people do not speak English, but we communicate by hand and foot. Still, I am somewhat alone in this country, and I would like to see you once more. We could make a walk to another end of the world."

There was a space and then this ending: "I am praying for you and does me remember everyday your person. God will provide. His ways are strange and wonderful."

For several more months I heard nothing from Abel. Then I received a letter from Archangel'sk, Russia, where Abel had a contract to build another brick factory. At the end of the letter, he wrote of his abandoned factory in San Chang: "We must believe that not all our works are worthlessness but not always we will see the harvest. On this earth all our doings will be done and accompanied with faults. But look to the best and never do forsake. . . ."

Accompanying his letter was another portion of his essay. It read:

> There is a magic in the marriage of clay and fire, or so it is and sometimes seems. Even if one is a professional ceramicist, it is still amazing and thrilling to find that it is possible to take a sticky, dirty, slimy substance that is generally considered worthless, or at best a nuisance, and turn it into an object of art. This does, indeed, seem magical.
>
> This magical transformation of clay into an artificial product, a demand KKK-product, is not easily attainable. It lies hidden beneath a mass of technical jargon, which must be studied and digested in some manner to obtain a first success. After the first successes, however, the floor of the laboratory will often be littered with the

fragments of your failures, smashed in anger and frustration. But you can learn a great deal from failure, provided you can face it.

The same is valid for the marketing team. Never be afraid of loss of face. If you feel that at first you cannot do it, the best antidote is to indulge yourself dramatically in an ecstasy of self-pity, curse your tools and your kiln for conspiring against you, and even your team, smash a few more samples of trials (preferably the bad ones).

But then, after the restoration of your mind, lift your head resolutely above the dismay and the shards, pick up the pieces, and go back to your work. Having rid yourself of frustration (and experimental products), you can go back to the business of experimentation, examining your mistakes and learning your art.

Being through this process repeatedly and having managed to retain your love for ceramics and your sense of humour, because of every mistake you have made you have also made a discovery that led you to more daring experiments. And from it all you can glean those technical skills that make advancements possible.

A few weeks later, another letter arrived, also from Archangel'sk, Russia. In it, Abel enclosed the final paragraphs of his essay on the art of ceramics:

> Forming clay, creating something that has form and beauty (KKK-tile) is a fever in the blood, but one that is deeply satisfying to the soul and pleasing to the eye. Yours and the buyers of the product. Some catch it; some are immune. And usually those who catch it cannot help but feel that those who are immune are also a little deprived.
>
> Only with passion for ceramics and the willingness to develop your own experience, and this while carrying your responsibility, will you obtain the necessary expected success. . . .

When I visited China the next summer, I asked one of the university drivers to take me to San Chang to collect my things. Abel had written to tell me he had returned briefly to San Chang to carry forward his work on the factory under the auspices of a different company, but the venture hadn't been a success. He had reinstated Farmer Wang as the faithful and reliable inspector of clay, but the local managers on the Chinese side had been impossible, and the Party secretary more wary than ever of Abel's direction. As Abel explained to me in his letter, though San Chang seemed remote from politics, the village was not immune to the wave of repression and suspicion that followed in the wake of the June Fourth tragedy.

I didn't know what to expect from San Chang when the university car pulled up to Abel's living quarters. Would the rooms be deserted, with the feel of a haunted house? My blue, white, and red-striped bags—bags familiar to all travellers in China—stood alone in the middle of Abel's empty rooms. Only a stray towel, accidentally left behind by a last-minute washer, lay on the cement floor. I looked inside the bag. The miniature Chinese screen was there and the cloisonné swan intact. But deep inside the bag I found a small box I did not remember packing. Curious, I dug it out and opened the flaps.

There sat serenely a small clay pot, roundly perfect. Inside the pot, someone had tucked a note that read:

> This hand-made pot is a very primitive piece of work. It is the result of a conversation we had when I showed you the first hand-made tiles in Hefei Three Factory (Jian Cai San Chang).
>
> This is the first pot I made in China. The moulding and shaping of it reminded me of something I once read, a story about the Dajaks told by a missionary. As by the Dajaks in Borneo a person dies deep in the jungle and far from his homeland, it is said that his soul will keep wandering about the country. In order to avoid

that his soul will take revenge, a magician conjures this soul up, puts it in a little ceramic pot and covers it up cautiously. Such a pot (*zielepotje/soulpot*) outstrips with all its primitive power the naive frills of our Western civilization.

The missionary tells how happily people lived there, out in the jungle. He talks a lot about very plain and simple things of daily life, instead of what you may expect from a disciple of Jesus Christ. You just feel this man to be an instrument in the hand of God. You often notice that people who do a lot of good things talk about their achievements only in understatements. One might come to the conclusion that on one's way to God, the mind might be the thing that prevents him from getting there. . . . Hefei, 03-06-89

I stroked the smooth surface of the clay pot, placed it back in its box, and sat down on the floor. Outside, the driver waited for me, but, drunk on memories, I could not move from the spot. Abel's rooms seemed alive with the ghosts of the past: Farmer Wang, Mr. Qu, and Abel himself. I could almost hear their distinctive steps as they trod down the cement-floored hallway. If only I could visit Farmer Wang and his family, I would feel better, I thought. If only I could watch the fires being stoked in the kilns, or listen for a while to the clank and rattle of the work in the brickyard, I could drown out the silence of Abel's Hefei Three Factory and assuage the aching sadness I felt as I surveyed its closed doors and boarded-up windows.

My driver, Mr. Lu, honked the horn. I knew he wanted to return to the university campus before dark, so I closed the door, locked it, and hurried down the stairs. Reluctantly, I climbed into the back seat of the car, placing my striped bags beside me. We pulled away from the factory and drove out through the gates of San Chang, with their bold announcement of the name of the village in Chinese characters forged from metal and painted red. As

I turned to catch one last glimpse of the factory, I recalled Abel's words, words etched deeply in my memory, as if inscribed on a clay tablet: "We must believe that not all our works are worthlessness but not always we will see the harvest. On this earth all our doings will be done and accompanied with faults. But look to the best and never do forsake. . . ."

The Evergreen Commune

IN LATE FEBRUARY, Xiao Li, a friend of Dan, took us, the foreign teachers, on our first official visit to a Chinese commune. As we turned off the main road onto a dirt road to our right, she pointed jubilantly ahead. The Evergreen Commune was the complete antithesis of its name. Before us stretched a vast panorama of desolation: not a green leaf, let alone a tree, broke the bleakness of the scene. If any colour should have been used to describe the barren world we encountered as we bumped down the dirt road on our bicycles, it would have been brown. And as I found out from Xiao Li, the evergreen trees alluded to in the name of the commune were not even indigenous to the region. The soil of this terrain nurtured only deciduous trees, which had been robbed of their leaves long ago by autumn winds, announcing to the stalwart inhabitants of the commune the advent of another bitter winter.

If the name of the commune was intended to have a metaphorical meaning, it was also a misnomer. Or if, after the fashion of socialist realism, it had been chosen to evoke

181

visions of the bright and prosperous future that lay at the end of the correct socialist path, in this sense, too, the name was ill suited to the place. Neither Arcadia nor Eden, the Evergreen Commune did not even rank as a paradise of the socialist sort in which the Tree of Knowledge would be firmly rooted in the soil of human self-reliance and snakes invited, even recruited, to contribute to the work of building up the new society by catching mice and other rodents.

A conversation I struck up with a middle-aged peasant woman labouring with her hoe in the fields reinforced the visual bleakness of the scene. I never anticipated that my casual remarks about China's economic growth and agricultural reforms would be greeted with a volley of bitter complaints about the thanklessness of physical labour and the poverty of a farmer's life. As if to illustrate her point, across the dirt road from us two men laboured, engaged in the sisyphean task of filling in a small pond by ferrying piles of dirt, loaded shovel by painstaking shovel, in a single wheelbarrow and dumping them into the water.

Xiao Li, our guide, was a tall and exceedingly beautiful young woman of about twenty. Though she had no formal connections with our university, she had attached herself to Dan, a tall, handsome, and boyish-looking man of about fifty, a professor of religion. She had met Dan at the opening of a local disco over which we, the foreign teachers, had been officially invited to preside. A confirmed bachelor who had recently taken his elderly and infirm mother into his home in Seattle, he was not a promising candidate for the suit of Xiao Li, whose family fully supported her by wooing him with elaborate dinners. But Xiao Li persisted, organizing our visit to the Evergreen Commune in yet another bid to gain Dan's favour. As we stopped in front of the commune's new brick factory, Xiao Li perched daintily on the seat of her bicycle, holding her handlebars with hands adorned by black lace gloves, a thin barrier between her delicate flesh and the bitter world.

Her English was poor, as Xiao Li herself kept telling us. Nevertheless she sallied forth, citing for our edification the kind of facts and figures Chinese tour guides love: the number of people living on the commune; how many hectares of land the commune comprised; how many factories it ran; how much the quota for production in each factory had increased in the past ten years; how many workers laboured in each factory; and on and on. If it hadn't been so cold, we might have nodded off to sleep in the course of Xiao Li's earnest speech. Instead, we stamped our feet and rubbed our hands together, relieved when her discourse ended and Xiao Li called us all to pose for a photo with some of the factory's sullen, bedraggled workers. A few schoolchildren, who had been quietly following us since we entered the commune, looked on, wide-eyed and silent.

While the workers stumbled, like somnambulists, back to the work of brick producing—the photo having served, they made you feel, as a momentary respite in their numb lives from the torments of the damned—the children drew away from us into an animated world of their own. As they left behind the constraints imposed upon them by their proximity to us, foreigners some and adults all, they began to run and shout, laughing with wild hilarity and taunting us to catch them if we could. Down a lane lined with waving willow trees which, though barren, shone golden in the noonday sun, across the bridge they ran, to the farthest reaches of the commune.

Suddenly, Dan hopped onto his bicycle and began to ride with all his might. I followed closely behind him as Xiao Li stood frozen in disbelief, wondering what was happening to our official tour. The other foreign teachers rode along behind us down the treacherously potholed dirt road as Xiao Li closed ranks, trying in vain to maintain a feminine pose as she lurched along its deeply rutted surface.

Following the now-screaming children, Dan disappeared from sight behind a row of adobe houses to the left.

Cows lowed. Chickens squawked. On a warmer day, the lane would have been lined with curious faces by now. I followed Dan to the very end of the courtyard where he stood straddling his bicycle, attempting to communicate with two groups of dumbstruck children as they peeked out from behind the doorways of the last two houses in the row. Before long, an elderly woman and a middle-aged one came to one door, then two more women and a man to the other. They smiled with open faces and admonished the children to come out and greet the foreign guest and welcome him inside.

By this time, Xiao Li had arrived. She began conversing in Chinese with the two families, explaining who we were. She told the curious peasants which countries we were from and what subjects we taught at the university. Then she translated for us a few facts about them. The name of the peasant family was Zhang, and all the families in the row of adobe houses were Zhangs and related. Xiao Li passed a few more minutes in polite conversation, with the rest of us trying out a Chinese word or two, before announcing our departure.

The Zhang family would not hear of it. It was time for lunch. We must all stay for a meal. Diplomatic enough to violate even this cardinal rule of Chinese peasant hospitality—that a guest should never leave your home hungry—Xiao Li made some excuse, explaining that a banquet had been prepared for us at the university and we were obligated to be there. It wasn't true, of course, but it allowed everyone to save face. Before leaving, we posed for a photograph with all the Zhangs outside one of their family homes. As we rode off, the Zhangs called out for us to visit again, next time for dinner.

Three months later, on the first Sunday in May, Sun Li and I decided to take a bicycle ride through the countryside to the south of the city. We didn't intend to visit the Evergreen Commune, but as we cycled down the busy highway, I recognized the dirt road leading to it and decided to show Sun Li around. Coming from the large industrial city of Shenyang, she knew as little about agricultural communes as I did—possibly even less, since now I had Xiao Li's official tour behind me. I doubted Sun Li would be interested in visiting the brick factory, so I swerved right, in the direction of the Zhang home. After all, the family had invited us to visit again, and I knew Chinese peasants sincerely meant their offers of hospitality. I was sure the Zhangs had been waiting to see us.

As Sun Li and I rode down the lane to the Zhang enclave, the children ran to meet us. The news of our coming had been carried, like pollen, through the fragrant spring air. By the time we brought our bicycles to a stop in front of the last Zhang dwelling, Mrs. Zhang had begun cleaning a freshly slaughtered chicken for our dinner. We stepped into the Zhang house. Since it was Sunday, the whole family was at home, three or four generations. The older children amused themselves trying to talk with us, while the Zhang grandmother minded the baby, and the men of the household slouched on wooden benches, smoking.

Mrs. Zhang ushered Sun Li and me to the family table at the far end of the large room. At the opposite end of the room, an earthen stove, fuelled by firewood, served as the only source of heat in the house. Mrs. Zhang's wok sizzled on top of it as she stir-fried the chopped vegetables. She signalled to her daughter to bring us glasses of steaming hot milk and a large jar of refined sugar, a delicacy for Chinese peasants, to sweeten it. Meanwhile, the eldest daughter brought us sunflower seeds and peanuts to tide us over until dinner time.

I had no intention of staying for dinner, I explained to Sun Li. I had only wanted to say hello to the Zhangs and to show her the commune. I had student papers to mark, and, besides, I didn't want to put the family to the trouble and expense of preparing a large meal. After we had drunk our milk and passed half an hour in stilted conversation,

Sun Li translating my questions and the Zhangs' answers, we thanked the family for their hospitality and rose to leave.

As we walked towards the door, Mrs. Zhang flew from her vegetable chopping to block our way, the smile never leaving her face. She shouted something to the children in Chinese. Before Sun Li could translate for me, the children had grabbed the bicycle key from my hand and run as fast as they could in the direction of the open fields. Another group of Zhang children quickly banded together to carry the bicycle itself away. As it disappeared behind the Zhang dwelling, I stared at Sun Li in disbelief. "I am afraid you must stay for dinner," Sun Li told me quietly. "If you don't, it will be a tragedy."

When I looked again at Mrs. Zhang's smiling and determined face, I knew Sun Li was not exaggerating. I settled back into my place at the wooden table. Mrs. Zhang resumed her chopping, the little boys gathered firewood, and the grandmother nodded, the leathery skin of her nut-brown face exploding into a hundred wrinkles as she smiled at the little Zhang daughter who gaily peed on the earthen floor of the home through her "split pants." The chicken cooked in the pot. What could Sun Li and I do but make ourselves at home?

The afternoon passed quickly, talk becoming sparser as Sun Li and I settled into the life of the family. We played with the children, minded the baby, collected a little firewood, and, with the youngest of the Zhang fathers, took a short tour of the plot of land he worked for the commune. When we returned, the eldest Zhang daughter wove a garland from the willow branches and spring flowers we had collected during our tour. When she had finished, she approached me, smiling, with downcast eyes, and placed it on my head.

The Zhang family had never entertained a foreigner before. To them, I must have seemed more strange than a spirit, some earth goddess the children might have imagined rising up out of the soil in the fields one misty morning. Now I wore the very crown of spring. All the Zhang children gathered around me giggling, and Sun Li insisted on taking a picture of me with the floral wreath poised on my head.

When, at last, Mrs. Zhang served the dinner of fresh chicken, vegetables, eggs, rice, and fried nuts, the children only picked at their own plates. They were too interested in watching me eat to care much about their own food. They monitored each mouthful, asking me about each dish and urging me to take more. The Zhangs asked nothing of me, except that I share their meal and teach their bright-eyed little boy of eight—obviously the darling of the clan—to speak a few words of English. But the boy, not the slightest bit interested in the family's plans for his education, continued to play games such as "How many peanuts can you balance between your chopsticks?"

After dinner, Sun Li nudged me gently. We had an hour's bicycle ride ahead of us, and already it was growing dark. Satisfied now, the Zhangs accepted my inevitable departure, but urged me, before I left, to come for a minute into the only other room in the small dwelling, a sparsely furnished bedroom. I wondered who, of all the many Zhangs present, slept in the large double bed. Mr. Zhang waved me in the direction of a small bureau by the window. At least a hundred Mao buttons of different sizes and designs were pinned to a cloth draped over it. He motioned to me to pick one. I shook my head, explaining that these buttons were valuable now, worth thirty American dollars or more each. As Sun Li translated my words into Chinese, Mr. Zhang shook his head and continued to gesture in the direction of the buttons.

Mrs. Zhang smiled and nodded her head with her eyes closed, as I had seen so many Chinese people do when they were being gracious to a visitor. By now I knew it was useless to try to contravene the will of the Zhang family, so I chose the plainest button, nodded my head, and bowed, thanking Mr. and Mrs. Zhang in Chinese for their kindness.

The whole family walked with Sun Li and me to the end of the Zhang enclave, where the dirt road began. As we rode off into the dusk, they waved us on. We turned around periodically to wave back until the family was just a silhouette of raised hands on a darkening horizon.

As we passed by the last field of the commune, I stopped to watch an old man harvesting sugar cane with a sickle. Sun Li pulled up beside me. The farmer's wide-brimmed straw hat and loosely fitting blue work clothes transported me back to Canada, and, for a moment, I was a child again on a summer visit to my grandmother's farm, and the figure receding against the darkening horizon was my grandmother, also a farmer who worked in the fields until dusk. I tried to convey to Sun Li the fleeting sensation. "You are homesick," she replied. "Let's go." Silently, we rode on into the dark night.

One day several weeks later, as I was lying in bed with a cold, Sun Li appeared at my door with a basket of fresh eggs on her arm and a small box filled with tea eggs.

"You shouldn't have!" I exclaimed.

"But they are not from me," Sun Li confessed. "Lao Zheng said a lady came by an hour ago, a peasant woman from the countryside, with these eggs. She said she knew you. Lao Zheng told her she must have the wrong place, but she insisted on leaving the eggs for you."

Sun Li and I looked at each other. "Mrs. Zhang!" we cried. Mrs. Zhang must have travelled by bus and then on foot for several miles to bring me the fresh eggs. Perhaps she had even heard I was sick? I felt badly that I hadn't been able to extend to her any hospitality after her long journey, and I decided that before I left China, I would cycle to the Evergreen Commune to take the Zhang family a small gift.

I set out one morning in late May. Sun Li was working, so I made the visit alone. The school year would officially end in June, and I was due to leave China in a few weeks. I knew this would be my last visit to the Evergreen Commune. As I rode down the busy highway to the outskirts of the city, I passed a home in which a Buddhist funeral ceremony was under way. Outside the home of the bereaved family, wreaths of paper flowers fluttered in the wind. Through the open door I saw family and friends gathered to pay their last respects.

But the countryside itself pulsed with life. Peasant men ploughed the rice paddies with their water buffalo, while the women ladled buckets of night-soil onto thriving vegetable patches. The poplar trees by the roadside swayed, their round leaves upturned by a warm gust of spring wind. At the commune, the golden willow trees, whose branches had been garnered to make a wreath for my head, almost hid the lane to the Zhang compound with their leafy, drooping branches. When I arrived at the Zhang home this time, no one noticed my coming. Everyone old and fit enough to work was busy with rice planting. The grandmother opened the door to welcome me in, offered me food and drink, then left me to myself as she minded the small baby.

I wanted to give the Zhangs a gift as exotic and precious to them as the Mao button was to me. I had searched the cupboards of my rooms. During the Spring Festival, I had travelled to India. In Maharashtra, I had bought some mirror-work from a local tribal people. My favourite piece, a large tapestry in an abstract design, portrayed a sunflower working its way out of the primeval darkness of earth into the glittering light of a thousand mirrors. I placed it on the Zhang bed and left.

I never knew what the Zhangs thought of the mirror-work, whether it conjured in their minds visions of a richer, better earth where life was easier and the sun always shone down on a world perpetually green. But I was sure that Mrs. Zhang had told her neighbours the story of the foreigner who had come to eat dinner in her home,

189

describing in detail how she had served a fresh chicken and many vegetable dishes and had given her a small present of eggs and a Mao button. I thought she might have boasted a little that the foreigner had promised to teach her son English and that the large piece of cloth, the one with the little glass pieces on it, had been brought as a gift from *waibian* (outside). To a close neighbouring family, she may have even prognosticated that the foreigner would be coming back next spring to visit the Evergreen Commune.

The Road to Anqing

"FOREIGNERS! FOREIGNERS!"—the word rings in the ears of any outsider who travels the road to Anqing. It's a long road, a dusty road. It leads to the Yangtze River and beyond, to the top of a holy Buddhist mountain, Jiuhua Shan. But the mountain is not important; it is the road that holds us, chokes us with its dust, accosts us with its wrinkled peasant women running behind our car, wagging their fingers as if to warn us that the road will change us and we will not return the way we came, on the road from Anqing.

The road begins in Hefei and passes through the heart of Anhui Province, once the poorest and now one of the most prosperous of China's agricultural provinces. Little towns like Feixi follow soon after. For hours, the countryside never really opens up its arms. A smattering of home-made brick kilns dots the fields. Everywhere, peasant villages are under construction. Factories grow up next to them. Industrial China emerges from the rice paddies. Occasionally, a bicyclist transporting geese in a basket passes. A brief stretch of verdure. The water buffalo heaves under its yoke. Then the dust rises up again and we choke.

The road to Anqing has few scenic views. Except *en route* to the Buddhist mountain, few from *waibian* (outside), pass here. To be "outside" here would mean dishonour; in the old days, it would even have meant death. Here, everyone belongs to someone. The man with the hunched back, the blind girl, all are part of the clan. Foreigners are a mere curiosity, not to be taken seriously.

We stop in a village, at the midway point of our journey. Our driver needs to eat *wufan* (lunch). He chooses one of the very rare roadside cafés. We have brought a lunch of bread, fruit, peanuts. We crouch for a roadside picnic. When we have finished eating, we set out to imbibe the cool, fresh air of the rice paddies, an undulating reprieve of green. First a small group of twittering schoolgirls detects us. They flutter, like timid birds, behind the long row of spindly poplar trees that separates the field from the road, then approach. As soon as they come close enough for us to speak to them, they fly away again, giggling shyly. A young mother holds up her child, as if to show him some scene of utmost importance. A tractor stops on the road. An elderly man backs up with his donkey and cart for a good view. We are unreal, images from the television screen that comes alive at night in the community hall. Where have they seen us before? In an American soap opera, or a cop show whose title the Chinese have translated as *Our Family Honour?* Some small boys draw boldly closer. They speak to us.

"Why do you eat your lunch on the roadside instead of in the café?"

"We like the scenery," we reply. "That is why we eat outside."

They laugh, incredulous. Why, they wonder, when you could be sitting inside the cosy tea-house? These foreigners, they do not care where they eat.

Beth's haircut, a short punk "do," acts as a magnetic

force. Head shaved closely except for a few stray tendrils at nape and forehead, she resembles a Buddhist nun. But her clothing—bright orange T-shirt and black-and-white polka-dot pants—shows she's not. The boys point to her hair and laugh. She points back at the same haircut, sported by an old man in the crowd. Everyone laughs again. These foreigners, they do not care what they wear.

But the road to Anqing doesn't always ring with laughter. It runs through a harsh land, stubborn, unpredictable. Factories, light industry, spring up beside ravaged gardens at the edge of peasant courtyards. Then, beyond, fields, endless fields, filled with farmers harvesting crops: tea, cotton, rice, peanuts. In the distance, brightly coloured shirts, pink and red, black hair against green, brown earth. Toil. The land stretches towards the horizon, hills fading into the background like the final stroke of a Chinese brush-stroke painting. Made for reverie. But who has time for dreaming here? The work goes on. The road to good health, to prosperity, to "lucky" is every inch a struggle for life.

The road to Anqing is filled with sorrow and with hope. We who pass through briefly, who are we to judge? Is the dust that flies everywhere a blessing or a curse? There is building. There is harvest. Who can lament the passing of old ways? The flooded banks of the Yangtze River burst in an effort to grasp what is already rushing downstream; an old river swells to embrace a newborn land. The road to Anqing does not end at the holy Buddhist mountain, where weary pilgrims, satchels of belongings over their shoulders, make their way, but high above the village of Jiuhua, in the terraced rice paddies, where no outsider dares to tread, where the golden harvest grows and the graves of the ancestors lie, well swept, serene, and undisturbed.

ANCIENT MUSIC

In China, a love of the beautiful endures. On the university campus where I taught, books, papers, and other essentials of academic life were in short supply, but carefully sculpted rock gardens and man-made ponds abounded. Lucid mirrors of weeping willow groves, these still ponds beckoned, their banks a favourite meeting place for students. There, underneath the willow trees, they practised their English lessons aloud in the early morning hours before classes. And there, once a week, they gathered for the English Garden, an hour of informal conversation between foreigners and other English speakers, a coveted opportunity for the students to look through China's open door to the West, where, for many, the hope of a graduate education lay. English—a distant and most beautiful music, echoing their new-found dreams.

Since the downfall of the Gang of Four in 1976, I was told, classical music has played alongside the traditional marching songs on the university's PA system. Today, the freshmen munch to the strains of Mozart blaring from the loudspeakers. Against the background of a delightfully ethereal flute concerto, the voice on the PA system shouts out political slogans and moral instructions. The melody reverberates in the crowded dining hall. Conversation ebbs and flows. A meditative hush descends upon the small groups eating their rice and their pork dumplings as the students stop and listen to the strains. Collecting cassette tapes is a passion for these students, and while rock and pop music are the most popular, a love of classical music also thrives.

The Shanghai Music Conservatory lies nestled in the heart of what was once the French Concession. Glimmerings of colonial grandeur still shine through the cheaply painted exteriors and dilapidated roofs. On the morning I arrived, a bass cellist from the Juilliard School in New York conducted a master class. Bass players had travelled days and nights on the notorious Chinese hard-seats to attend. The master interpreted works by Koussevitzky, Brahms, Tchaikovsky. One student player, a tall young man from Harbin, quickly understood his instructions. Face impassive, he corrected his bowing while the others looked on. Next year he will study at Harvard.

At the end of the class, the master reflected: "When I first came to China, I noticed that everyone was wearing the same clothes, and I said to myself that when the streets were full of colour, then the playing would be colourful too. Today, the streets of Shanghai are brilliant, and so are you!"

In my Shakespeare class one day, Miss Qu offered her interpretation of a well-known passage from Twelfth Night. *"Music is the food of love," she explained, "because although one can live without food, one cannot live without music."*

"Yes," piped up Mr. Chen, who then broke into a rousing chorus from Figaro *as the class filed out into the hall.*

At Fuyang Teachers' College, I had a brief moment to myself in the middle of a busy schedule. I sat alone in the classroom after the students had left and closed my eyes. Gradually, I became aware of the poignant trills of a violin. In the dormitory next door, a student played a tape of The Butterfly Lovers—*of all the music I had heard playing in campus dormitories in China over the months, the most popular piece.*

The concerto harmonizes Chinese and Western musical styles, and interprets an ancient Chinese legend about two lovers who renounce a life of separation for death, after which they are united as butterflies. The concerto brings the Chinese legend to Westerners, who are familiar with the form and the instruments, but it also frames the legend in a new way for the Chinese.

China remembers. The sleeping dragon awakens. A lost harmony re-establishes itself. Through the open door drifts an ancient music.

Revolutionary Heroes

LIN XIAOWU WAS A TEACHER at the Hefei Number Two Primary School. He had nothing to do with the university where I taught and no connection to me or my life, except an interest in Canada that he had nurtured successfully without my help for several years. But the second semester had already begun, and I had been in China long enough not to be surprised when a complete stranger appeared at my door intent on engaging me in a serious and often lengthy conversation.

Lin Xiaowu had two distinctions in life. The first was that he had translated the Canadian author Robert Kroetsch into Chinese. I can still see in front of me the photocopied title page of the Chinese version of *Badlands*, with its sketch of a lone cowboy riding across a desert landscape punctuated by a single lonely cactus. Why Lin Xiaowu had decided to translate this particular text was a mystery to me. I couldn't imagine anything less likely to grip the imagination of a primary-school teacher in China than this post-modernist tale of the Canadian West. What could have compelled him to dedicate himself to the labour of translating it for his people? Yet there it was, in shapely Chinese characters, beckoning the Chinese reader to a world far away.

Lin's other distinction was that he was writing a biography of a famous Chinese sculptor who lived in Beijing. He had met the famous artist through his brother, who was a painter. Lin had done all the research for the biography, he explained. But because such a book was critical to an understanding of Chinese culture by the West, he continued, it had to be written by a Westerner, someone who was sympathetic, who loved literature and art, and who could write well in English.

"A very good idea," I said, not addressing his oblique query. "I wish you every success with your project." I offered Lin more tea, hoping he would take that as a cue to leave. He did not.

"When will you go to Beijing?" he persisted.

"I have no plans to go to Beijing at this time," I answered truthfully.

He continued, "But surely you will visit our capital city while you are in China?" Then he added, "Did I mention that I am starting a publishing company and could publish the book myself?"

I didn't hear from Lin for several months. Then in late April, a week before I was to travel to Beijing for a job interview, Lin dropped by again. "I hear you are travelling to Beijing next week," he said.

By now I had been exasperated far too many times by the leakage of information about my personal life to be irritated by his remark. "Yes," I said simply. "That is true."

"Then I hope you will meet my friend, the famous sculptor. I have already written to tell him you are coming. Here is his card. His address and phone number are on the front. Just call when you arrive in Beijing to arrange the interview."

With a few more words about his latest translation work

and a pitch for his fledgling publishing company, Lin left my rooms, never to be seen in the Foreign Guest-house again.

Lin had won. I couldn't refuse. I had no idea why I should meet the famous sculptor, let alone write a biography of him. As far as Chinese art went, I was an amateur. Still, I had always been drawn to its beauty. I recalled a childhood yearning to reproduce the simple, serene landscapes of Chinese brushstroke paintings in endless ink sketches of moons framed by plum branches, two swans swimming neck and neck in a still pond beneath them. I also remembered how, much later, as a university student, I had lost myself in Yeats's "Lapis Lazuli," following his three glittering-eyed Chinese men up the mountain to that halfway house, framed by cherry blossoms, mountain, and sky, where, looking down upon the tragic scene below, one of them would, with deft fingers, play mournful melodies on his *pipa*. More recently, I had experienced the joy of my first successes at Chinese calligraphy. Characters like *fu* (happiness) and *shou* (longevity) now hung on the walls of my rooms. But had any of this prepared me for meeting a famous Chinese sculptor?

On my last day in Beijing I called the sculptor's home. A woman answered. She set the appointment for three o'clock that afternoon. I would stop in on my way to the train station. The elderly sculptor lived at the centre of old Beijing, down a little alley called May Fourth Lane, not far from Tiananmen Square. The door to his home was unprepossessing. Who would imagine it would open onto another world? As I stepped over the thick-bottomed doorway common in Chinese homes of previous centuries, a delicate, white-haired woman of some refinement bowed slightly as she said in a melodious Beijing accent, "Please come in."

I stood inside a small, sunny courtyard. Sliding wooden doors painted a deep russet red blocked off the various rooms of the house. The white-haired lady, the aging sculptor's wife, walked in small, staccato steps in front of me, as if she were playing on the set of a Peking Opera. She led me through an open door. Along the wall facing the door stretched a comfortable-looking divan. I seated myself and waited for my host. From where I sat, adjacent to the open door, I could see across the courtyard into a large, high-ceilinged room where a band of white shapes, cut from stone, crowded together as if in earnest conversation.

"Bonjour," said the sculptor in chaste and lucid Parisian French as he entered the room. "Won't you please make yourself at home?" he said, waving his hand towards the tea and cakes his wife was laying out on the table.

As I reached for a cake, it occurred to me how generous he had been in inviting me to his home. A sculptor of national and international renown, he must have had many requests from visitors wanting to interview him. What presumption Lin had had, I reflected, to think I could write a biography of this enigmatic man, who had witnessed the birth and the death of worlds, the rise and fall of empires and regimes, before I had even been born.

We chatted about the French language, marvelling at its many permutations throughout the world and comparing our own two variations: his Parisian French and my own patois learned during summers in rural Quebec. Gradually, we approached more serious subjects: philosophy, politics, religion. The conversation carried us, as if on wings. We circled above whole worlds of thought.

"Yes, Jesus, Buddha, Muhammad, Karl Marx—all were teachers," the sculptor responded in an urbane and tolerant voice to my questions about China, religion, and the ideologies of the West.

Finally, we touched on the sculptor's life in the Paris of the 1930s. From our conversation, I imagined a young man of refinement, hair combed back, wandering the Louvre, drinking tea and smoking endless cigarettes in cafés on the Left Bank, discussing with his confrères his new experimental art. I imagined the young idealist lying awake at night in a narrow cot in a small crowded room, dreaming of how art might be married to political ideology. It hardly seemed germane to ask the question now, and yet the memory of Lin Xiaowu, his earnest eyes looking at me hopefully as he told me about his plans to start a publishing company, compelled me to say, "I would like to write a biography of you, Monsieur."

The sculptor paused for a moment, then smiled and replied, "That would be very difficult."

I said nothing more on the subject. The afternoon light grew bright then soft. It was almost time for me to catch my train back to Hefei. "Before I go," I asked, "may I see your studio?"

He nodded and, without a word, led me to the room across the courtyard. We passed through an open sliding door into a spacious, high-ceilinged room equipped with all the instruments of the sculptor: plaster, moulds, cement blocks, mallets, chisels, saws, blades, and knives. The torsos and heads of figures of state—past leaders of China, Party secretaries, mayors—lay strewn about the floor. At the centre of the crowd loomed a gargantuan figure cut from white stone and close to completion—a soldier, perhaps some obscure revolutionary hero.

I stood and stared, pondering the identity of these larger-than-life figures. The sculptor ambled about the room looking almost quizzically at his creations. Surrounded by the crowd of lifeless figures, I felt as if the ghosts of a past world attended us. It was as if the figures were, in response to all the questions I had asked of their maker, crying out at me in recrimination: "What do you know? Where were you then?"

As a final courtesy, the sculptor gave me a book, written in Chinese, on his life and art. On the first page, he inscribed his best wishes and, beneath them, my Chinese, not my English, name: Hu Jin Le. As I stepped through the doorway into May Fourth Lane and climbed into the waiting taxi, I felt as if I had re-entered the world of time.

Here, there were a train to catch, classes to teach, and traffic to avoid.

On the way to the station, we passed Tiananmen Square. The day I arrived in Beijing the city streets had been teeming with protesters marching for democracy, all of them converging on the square. But today, the square was almost empty. Only a few children with their parents flew dragon-kites in the fading light. In the distance towered the Monument to the People's Heroes. Engraved on its sides were the revolutionary martyrs, sleepless, vigilant, in perpetual struggle against class-enemies and their offspring: oppression, famine, and war.

On past visits to the square, I had studied the panels closely. I remembered some of them well. One depicted a scene from the Opium Wars; another, the May Fourth student demonstrations in 1919 against the Treaty of Versailles; and another, the war against Japan. Some of the figures, too, were familiar, especially the young woman harvesting wheat for soldiers at the front, and the young soldier gazing at a distant shore as he forded the Changjiang River with his PLA cohorts during a successful campaign against the Guomindang. While all China slept, the revolutionary martyrs kept eternal vigil.

The centrepiece of revolutionary China, the brainchild of a young artist who had studied in the twilight gaiety of Paris as the Great Depression descended, the sculpture, a massive piece of stone—how many tons?— gleamed in the intense and revealing light of the setting sun. It towered above the square, pristine, white, beautiful. No legends of spilt blood had yet stained its purity. No bullets had chiselled their way into the fine, noble features of its young heroes and heroines. No tanks had inscribed their vicious tread on the stones of the square where the heroes reigned supreme, triumphant. No goddess of democracy, made of white plaster and youthful idealism, yet overshadowed it.

Just then the monument stood not totally pure but in

relative innocence, a monument radiating good intentions, a vision set in stone for all the world to see: revolutionary heroes caught up in a dream doomed to take shape as a recurrent nightmare until a new world would finally lay it to rest. It had taken me some time to perceive this truth, a truth the elderly sculptor and perhaps even Lin Xiaowu had probably understood long ago.

Elsa's Paintings

ELSA'S ROOM WAS COVERED with mountains. It hadn't always been that way. When I passed through Shanghai on my way to Hefei in September, Elsa was sharing her room at the music conservatory with a young diva of the Peking Opera, a Dutch girl with a wild mane of red hair who strode down the halls singing, full-throatedly, her arias. The arrangement was doomed from the start. Elsa needed room to spread out; Tikka needed space to sing. When I visited the conservatory a few months later, Tikka had moved in with Melanie, an English woman whose studies of Chinese, a language she was learning solely in order to communicate with her Chinese fiancé who was studying in San Francisco, were tinged with desperation and, at times, even despair.

"Why don't you go and join him in San Francisco?" I asked Melanie. "You can speak English together there. Why do you stay?"

"When I go to the cinema and hear the old men spitting," she explained, "I just say to myself, 'I love China.' "

Melanie was definitely a more suitable roommate for Tikka. Already inseparable, they were settling happily into their life together in Shanghai. Elsa had to pay an extra forty *yuan* a week to have a room to herself. But it was worth it. All over the bed where Tikka had once slept, Elsa had spread out her highest-quality rice paper for painting, as well as other, lower-grade brands of paper marked off in squares for the practice of calligraphy.

Elsa was an artist from San Francisco, an "abstract expressionist," as she described herself. She had left China several times in utter frustration, but each time, as soon as she had boarded the outbound plane, she was already restless to return. During her two years in Shanghai, Elsa had understood many things about China. She told me about what she called "the great walls of China," meaning the frustration of endless bureaucracy, and she explained to me that in China, because life was so slow, I would have time to think. "About what?" I asked.

"Oh, about everything. . . ," she mused. She also expressed her conviction that those of us who had come to China from the outside must be like bridges, living in two worlds at once and serving as a link between them. To me, it sounded impossibly idealistic.

A few weeks after my last visit with her, I received a letter from Elsa. She needed some rice paper—a special kind called Xuanzhou Paper, made only in Anhui Province—for a show she was preparing, a joint art venture with a Chinese painter she had met through her calligraphy teacher. I cycled all over town showing shopkeepers the small piece of paper Elsa had sent me with the name of the brand inscribed on it in Chinese characters. No one had heard of a special brand of rice paper made only in Anhui Province.

In January, I received a small package from Elsa. Enclosed was an invitation to the opening of her new show, "Elsa Marley, Chen Keliang – Joint Venture." A brochure described Elsa's philosophy of art: "I believe the nature of pure Art lies in universality. To venture into the unknown, the universal, is part of the Artist's task." The brochure went on to say that through the process of artistic exchange, both artists had come "one step closer to the top of the mountain wherein lies . . . the universality of the unknown."

In her package, Elsa also enclosed a small piece of calligraphy in her own hand, which I hung on my wall. My Chinese students told me it read "Happy Birthday" and that even though it was obviously by a foreigner, it wasn't a bad piece of calligraphy at all. At the very bottom of the package, I discovered a T-shirt with the logo of the show on it, "West Mountain," bordering a boldly expressionist rendering of the same mountain.

I didn't make it to Elsa's show. I had just returned from India, where I had spent the Spring Festival vacation, and I was still recovering from the bronchitis I had caught in Bombay. I had flown from Bombay to China in only ten hours, but it had taken me another two days to get from Nanjing to Hefei, a four-hour train trip. I was not in the mood to travel anywhere. In March, Elsa wrote again to tell me the show had gone well. People from the embassies and local artists as well as some well-known Chinese painters had come. The show had received positive reviews in Chinese and English newspapers.

I didn't visit Shanghai again until May. The day after I arrived, I went to look for Elsa. I knocked on the door of her room at the conservatory. A stranger answered.

"Elsa?" I asked.

"Elsa's down there," the woman said, pointing to the end of the hall.

I thanked her and walked down the hall to Elsa's new room. I knocked and Elsa opened the door. Unlike her previous room, this one was situated so that the building adjacent to the dormitory didn't block the sunlight. The light of the midday sun streamed into the room, illuminating the scrolls that hung on every inch of each wall and lay rolled out on every available surface.

Except for Elsa herself, the room betrayed no sign of a human presence: it pulsated with the muted chiaroscuro elegance of Chinese brushstroke paintings, which rendered, in all their primeval holiness, the haunting beauty of various Buddhist mountains. No figures populated these landscapes. The mountains stood alone—remote, serene, unapproachable. Scenes of unearthly grandeur, they looked almost like temples to the great cosmic force that made them, whatever be its name: Tao, Brahman, the Great Spirit, Allah, God.

"Come in!" Elsa said, hugging me. "What do you think?"

"They're beautiful!"

"Chen says I will have to learn more about the brush," Elsa continued, "but he is happy with them."

"They're neither walls nor bridges," I observed. "They're something altogether different."

"Yes," Elsa laughed, "they're mountains!"

I didn't see Elsa again before I left China in June 1989. But not long after I arrived back in Canada, I received a letter from her. It had been forwarded from my university in China, and it bore a Chinese postmark. In it, Elsa told me she had decided to leave Shanghai when protesters had set fire to a train in the dark, angry days after the Tiananmen tragedy.

Elsa did not say where she had gone, and I could not decipher the original postmark under the Chinese one stamped on for forwarding. But somehow I imagined Elsa still in China, in a quieter place, far from a major city, a lone figure eternally wandering in the mountains or maybe walking hand in hand with her Chinese painter friend in the cool chiaroscuro of a brushstroke-painting dawn.

Monkey King's Journey to the Middle East Kingdom

THE MONKEY KING is an incurable trickster. No matter how obedient he may appear at a given moment, you can never really trust him. The monk Tripitaka learned this the hard way when he took the Monkey King on his journey to the West. When Tripitaka found him, the Monkey King was a prisoner in the Mountain of Two Frontiers. He had been waiting five hundred years for Tripitaka to come and was delighted to see him at last, recognizing in his arrival the fulfilment of Guanyin's promise that he was destined to earn his salvation by accompanying a monk on his travels to India to fetch the Buddhist scriptures.

"Get me out of this mountain," the Monkey King cried to Tripitaka. Once Tripitaka removed Buddha's golden-lettered seal and released the Monkey King from his mountain prison, he had no end of trouble. Unruly in his appetites and quick-tempered, Tripitaka's disciple needed constant discipline. To help in the process, Guanyin gave Tripitaka an embroidered cap with bands of inlaid gold in it that hurt the Monkey King's head whenever Tripitaka recited the "Headband Spell."

Perhaps it is because of this interesting twist in his nature that the Monkey King is one of the best-loved characters in Chinese opera. After all, an excess of passion and imagination is one of the most endearing of all human vices. An opera called *The Magic Palm Fan* gives some idea of the boundless energy and ingenuity of the Monkey King and shows just how challenging he found it to control his passions and use his imagination—symbolized by his formidable magic powers—only for good. The plot is drawn from one of the episodes in the classic novel *Journey to the West.*

Tripitaka and his three disciples—the Monkey King, Pigsy, and Sandy—are travelling through a very hot pass near the Flame Mountain of the West. The heat is unbearable, but Tripitaka and his three disciples must journey through it since the pass is the only way to India and the Buddhist scriptures. So the Monkey King devises a scheme: he will borrow a magic fan from a fairy to put out the flame heating the mountain.

Laying on his usual charm, the Monkey King attempts to woo the fairy into giving him the fan. He affectionately calls her "sister-in-law," but she is not taken in. Instead of warming up to the Monkey King, she accuses him of defeating her son in battle. Drawing upon his magic powers, the Monkey King then changes himself into a fly and drops into her teacup. Once in her stomach, he causes her so much pain that she agrees to give him the fan. But the one the fairy gives him is a fake, and the Monkey King is forced to try another ploy.

Next, the Monkey King consults with Ox, the fairy's husband. Ox refuses to help, but, as a result of meeting him, the Monkey King gets an idea for a new plan: he will transform himself into Ox. Once he does, the fairy not only gives the Monkey King the fan but gives him a magic spell that will make the fan grow large enough to put out the fire heating Flame Mountain. After a brief battle with Ox, who suspects his ruse, the Monkey King returns to Flame Mountain and extinguishes the fire so he and his fellow-travellers can continue their journey.

But the adventures of the Monkey King are not the only subject of Chinese opera. I remember attending a performance showcasing various amateur Huangmei Opera troupes, in a small low-ceilinged building down a dark lane in Hefei. Anqing, not far from Hefei, is the birthplace of one of the early forms of the Peking Opera, an opera remarkable for its colourful, fast-paced action punctuated by the sharp click of the clapper sticks.

The stories were elementary, even primitive, and filled with those crudely dramatic shifts of fate that make opera so compelling. One story had as its central character Bao Zheng, the celebrated honest official from Hefei who lived during the Northern Song Dynasty. The complication develops when Chen, a young man from the countryside, goes to the capital city to take the Imperial Examination. Chen not only passes the exam but becomes the Number One Scholar, a title conferred on the one who places first. As a result of his success in the examination, the emperor asks Chen to marry his daughter. Soon after, Chen's first wife, Qin, goes to the capital to look for her husband, taking her son and daughter with her. Chen not only refuses to admit he knows them, he goes so far as to plan to have them killed. Feeling pity for the young wife and her children, the hired killer does not execute the plan.

Eventually, Qin goes to Bao Zheng demanding justice. Bao Zheng takes Chen to court and questions him. Chen, thinking his position as the son-in-law of the emperor will protect him, is unrepentant. Angry, Bao Zheng decides to execute Chen. The emperor's mother and his daughter, Chen's new wife, both try to dissuade Bao Zheng from this course of action, but, valuing justice above all else, he carries out his verdict.

The men who watched the opera, all locals, sat on

wooden benches in loosely fitting cotton undershirts. Slouched over, they smoked cigarettes, spat on the floor occasionally, and muttered "hao!" (good), accompanied by surprised laughs. They might have seen this opera countless times before, but a sudden twist in the action—Qin's shrill cry on hearing Bao's judgement or the stunning acrobatics of Chen's struggle to escape—brought them unexpected delight.

Beth, myself, and Lin, a young friend of Beth whose father has written a book on the Huangmei Opera, were the only women in the room. When we arrived, the men stared at us in surprise and gossiped in low voices. The judges, who sat behind two long tables covered with white tablecloths, stopped sipping their tea and gazed in our direction for a minute. But after a while, the stares stopped and the talk died out. Everyone settled in to watch the performance, just an amateur production but with each player in the full costume of a character in one of the four categories in which each actor specializes: the *sheng*, the *dan*, the *jing*, or the *chou*.

The *sheng* character plays one of three roles: *lao sheng*, a bearded man past middle age; *xiao sheng*, a young man; or *wu sheng*, a military man played by an actor highly trained in acrobatics. The *dan* role is a female role and requires expertise in six main parts, ranging from the virtuous woman to the flirtatious woman and from the young, unmarried girl to the aging matron. The female warrior, or *dao ma dan*, is one of the most interesting female parts. She moves with military precision and wears a headdress with long pheasant feathers springing out of it, and four pennants strapped to her back and her *kao*, or armour.

But even more arresting, especially to the foreign eye, is the first sight of the *jing*, or the painted-face character. Playing a high-ranking army general, a warrior, or an official, the *jing* character swaggers onto the stage in his elaborate costume and ornate headdress, his face boldly painted in a complex design dominated by red if he is good, white if he is crafty or cunning, black if he is upright, and blue if he is wild. With his deep, gruff voice and his boldly painted face, he commands the stage in every scene he plays.

The *jing* forms a stark contrast to the *chou* character— the rogue, the scholar, and the prince. Of all the *chou* characters, the Monkey King is most universally loved. Something in his quizzical animal smile, fierce independence, boundless ingenuity, and bold white and red face-paint captures the imagination. The heart of every opera lover always skips a beat when he appears on stage in his yellow, silken costume.

To play in the Chinese opera requires years of training. Most singers begin their apprenticeship to the art in early childhood. In the past, whole families made their living by practising the art. Some still do. In Hefei, I was invited one crisp autumn day to have lunch with one such opera family. I rode my bicycle to the southern part of the city and parked in front of an enclave where many of the city's 160-member opera troupe live. As I ate a delicious lunch of fish and vegetable dishes, I listened to the Wong family story.

Born in Beijing, the Wongs began their apprenticeship to the opera at the age of eight. All the Wongs' ancestors performed in the Peking Opera. The Wongs themselves learned the art from their parents and other relatives. Mrs. Wong studied with Dr. Mei Lanfang, a famous opera teacher from Beijing. She plays mostly the *dan* role. Mr. Wong plays the *chou* character, especially the Monkey King. Since childhood, the Wongs' lives have been ruled by a strict regimen: practice in the morning, rest in the afternoon, and performance in the evening.

During the Cultural Revolution, this regimen was modified, Political Study being intertwined with practice in the morning and hard labour supplanting rest in the afternoon. In those days, the Wongs rarely performed the traditional Peking Opera. Instead they sang songs popular at the time for the entertainment of officials and foreigners. The Wongs didn't choose their profession, they point out, but they love it anyway. It is, they explain, their way of life. Ever since they met and began singing together thirty years ago, they have made their living performing opera.

The Wongs' daughter is a part-time, amateur performer who occasionally volunteers to act on stage. With her parents' blessing and encouragement, she is treading the path of the new generation by studying English full-time. Also in keeping with the spirit of the times, the Wongs have translated a well-known Peking Opera into English—*Picking Up the Jade Bracelet*. Such a translation, the Wongs explain, will help the Chinese audience learn more about the English language through the medium of art. It will also help English speakers to appreciate the Peking Opera. In the translation, Mrs. Wong says, they took special care to harmonize the rhythms of the English language with the music of the Peking Opera.

Several weeks after my lunch with the Wongs, I was in Shanghai riding in a cab with a driver who happened to speak English. I asked him what he thought about the Wongs' plan to perform the Peking Opera in English. He told me it was good to translate the Chinese opera for English-speaking people so they could tell the Chinese how to do it better! I was astonished to discover that the popular conception of Western expertise extended even to the improvement of traditional Chinese art forms.

The weekend after I returned from Shanghai, I went downtown with Beth to see the Wongs' English-language opera premiered. A timeless piece about a love bond serendipitously forged, *Picking Up the Jade Bracelet* is a favourite among opera lovers. The opera begins with the accidental meeting of a girl feeding chickens in the yard of her home and a young scholar passing by. The scholar falls in love with the girl at first sight and presents her with a jade bracelet. Not wanting to seem bold, she rejects his gift, so he leaves it on the ground and disappears. After the scholar leaves, the girl picks up the bracelet. A go-between happens to be watching and arranges for the two to be married.

It was jarring to hear the characters articulating English phrases such as "Would you li–ike a cup of te–ea" to the plunk, plunk of the *erhu* and the click, click of the clapper sticks. But it did make the world of the Peking Opera seem a little less distant, exotic, and strange. Seeing the English-language version of this classic piece made me realize that despite the elaborate costumes, the stylized gestures and movements, the high falsetto voices issuing, as they seem to a Western audience to do, from behind lips tense with a curious form of emotional repression, the Peking Opera is not unlike a play by Shakespeare in its weaving of simple matters of the heart into gripping plots universal in their significance.

The last time I visited China I was too busy to attend operas. Running between conference sessions and the homes of friends, I didn't have time to think of dinner, let alone operas. As I sat waiting to board the homeward-bound plane to Israel, where I was living, I regretted the lost opportunity. To distract myself, I took a long look out the window of the boarding lounge, just to imprint on my mind one last view of China. Outside, the barren November fields surrounding the Beijing airport seemed to shiver under the austere regime of winter.

The boarding call came over the PA system, and what appeared to be a group of Chinese tourists on their way to Israel smiled their way past me as they boarded the plane. Young and fit, they seemed especially suited for hikes in the Galilee, dips in the Dead Sea, a climb up to Masada, and even an all-night vigil in the desert. I nodded to them as they passed, flashing visas to another kind of holy land than the one Tripitaka had sought. Then I boarded the plane myself.

It was early evening when we took off, so we flew mostly in darkness. I was in no mood to talk, so I curled up in my window seat and strained my eyes for some sign of the Gobi Desert below. I knew we were flying north, then south over Europe and on to the Mediterranean world of azure sea, emerald islands, blue sky. At dawn, I awoke to the buzz of low laughter and hushed conversation.

I opened my eyes. In front of me, in the aisle, stood the strangest and most delightfully furry creature. It was the Monkey King himself. The "tourists" I had seen were performers in the Heilongjiang Opera Troupe travelling to debut the Peking Opera in Israel. El Al flights between Tel Aviv and Beijing had begun in September, and it was only the end of November. The Monkey King had wasted no time.

I introduced myself to the Monkey King and watched him put the finishing touches on his makeup. The whole opera troupe followed suit. First the hair was pulled back and tucked under a white cap. Then the face was painted: a white mask at the base and brightly coloured face paint applied in various patterns, according to which character was being played, on top. Last came the costumes: the silken robes and high-platformed shoes of the courtiers and officials of ancient China. And, of course, the furry dress of the agile Monkey King in all his iconoclastic glory.

When the opera troupe played in Haifa several days later, I went to see the performance. The players invited me backstage to photograph them as they put on their makeup and costumes. We chatted some more. Since we had already met on the plane, we felt like fellow-travellers, both strangers and at home in this foreign land. The performance was a dynamic one, filled with the wild, fast-paced acrobatics that make the Peking Opera such an engaging art form. The troupe did some popular pieces, easily accessible to the audience, some of them based on episodes from *Journey to the West*. The Israeli audience loved them.

I had seen my Peking Opera in the end, and I hadn't even had to go to Beijing to do it. I was delighted by this fortuitous turn of events. It was the kind of twist you might find in the plot of the Peking Opera itself. But what I remember most about the visit of the Heilongjiang Opera Troupe to Israel was not its performance, but the moment, just as the sun was showering its first brilliant pink rays over desert sands that had known Moses, when the players disembarked from the plane.

High officials in the Israeli Ministry of Culture, opera lovers, artistic directors, and public relations people waited on the tarmac to greet the troupe. The sun's rays grew in intensity, shining brighter and brighter as if to illuminate old hieroglyphs and reveal ancient secrets anew. For a brief moment, I wondered if the Monkey King, still an incurable trickster, was playing a joke on us all, especially on the players of the Peking Opera.

I knew that the Heilongjiang Opera Troupe would enjoy touring Israel and performing in what, for many, is a holy land, but had the Monkey King, I wondered, told the players they were going on a journey to the "West"? In the rich, flowing silks and majestic headdresses of ancient China, the troupe descended the stairs of the ramp. The press rushed forward to catch the moment. Cameras flashed against the dawn. There was no turning back now: the Monkey King had arrived in the Middle East Kingdom.

A Necklace with Bright Pearls

I HAD BEEN LIVING IN Hefei for several months when I came across a glossy tourist booklet produced for visitors and prospective business people, entitled *Charms and Features of Hefei.* A crowded, polluted, medium-sized city with a modicum of sparkling new highrises and a plethora of bicycle-thronged streets filled with merchants hawking everything from succulent yellow-skinned Chinese pears to twirling birds on sticks for children, Hefei hardly seemed to me a place of note in China. But I had read enough Chinese tourist brochures to know that, written by some former English major whose ears still rang with the cadences of Shelley and Tennyson and whose pen wavered uncertainly between poetry and political correctness, they could be pure rhapsody. I opened the booklet and read with interest.

Since the agricultural reforms ten years ago, there had been "a marked development in the social economy of the countryside of Hefei," I learned. The Hefei Vegetable Company had achieved good results by "keeping neither a too firm nor a too loose hand on the management of farm produce and sideline products and organizing the supply carefully" and by "persisting in taking vegetables as the key link." Hefei, I gleaned from the barrage of statistics that followed, boasted, among other things, 97,944 live pigs, 2,190,000 domestic fowl, and a total annual yield of 142,167 tons of vegetables.

I had often bargained with leathery-skinned peasants for one *jin* of withered local apples, walking away, as my friends had told me to do, when the price was too high. But the watermelons, piled high on the roadside in the warm months, and the winter oranges that appeared just before Christmas—"mandarins," as I had grown up calling them—tasted even better than the ones I remembered from my childhood, and inevitably the straw-hatted peasants selling them would cajole me, with cries of "hen hao chi" (delicious) and "hen pianyi!" (very cheap!), into buying them, whatever the price.

I wondered if any of these were included in the "charms" of the city. I flipped to the list of Hefei's "special products." To my surprise, I found I had sampled many of the foods named there: for example, the sweet Feidong peanuts in the fried peanut snack Madame Liu sometimes served me after our Chinese lesson, and the celebrated "Imperial Tribute, Yaxue Polished Glutinous Rice" in the rice dish Wu Li had served me to celebrate the Mid-autumn Festival. And I had tried the "three best products of Wabuhu Lake"—the whitebait, shrimp, and mao swordfish—and the tasty duck, "Shanhe Duck" as it was called in ancient times, at the numerous banquets I had been invited to attend.

Still, in a contest of China's gastronomical delights, I doubted that a Feidong peanut would win over a Beijing Duck, its tender meat rolled up with greens inside a small pancake stuck together by a sweet, gooey bean paste. I thought there must be other more compelling "charms and features" to imprint the city of Hefei on the mind of the foreign traveller in China. I turned to the section on industry.

The development of industry, I learned to my chagrin, had "gone through a tortuous road." But, thankfully, now it was "soaring." The Hefei Vehicle Manufacturing Plant was "advancing with giant strides in the course of reform," and, recently, a "Flower Spray," the Hefei Refrigerator Factory, had sprung up in the city. I had had no firsthand experience of Hefei's industries, but I knew that the Swedish businessmen who congregated each afternoon for drinks in the lobby of the Luyang Hotel called China the *meiyou* (not have) country. And they had told me that a New York Jew, who also lived in the hotel, periodically vented his frustrations over doing business with the Chinese by blowing a horn out his window in the early morning hours.

I found out from reading the booklet that the banks, too, flourished as they underwent various kinds of reforms and collected "funds to serve construction and support the four modernizations." And thanks to the Hefei Insurance Company, insurance was "entering millions upon millions of households like an auspicious bird." I had learned something about the world of Chinese commerce when I had filled out numerous forms to change a traveller's cheque worth only twenty dollars into Chinese currency at a local Bank of China. As for insurance, I understood why it had become so popular. During my first foray outside the city my driver had barrelled at high speed down the very centre of the potholed highway, dipping to the right only to avoid an oncoming car or truck and to the left only to skirt around a cyclist loaded down with a basket full of geese.

Industry and commerce could hardly develop without efficient transportation and communication systems, I thought, so I turned next to these sections. Hefei's Luogang Airport, I discovered, ranked as one of China's ten most modern airports and served as an ideal place "for any kind of international airliners to land when in an emergency." And now, since the advent of long-distance direct-dialling, Hefei, a city previously "riddled with gaping wounds," had become the "hub of communication of the province."

I had had considerable experience with China's transportation and communication systems. For example, I had often ridden to the centre of the city on crowded, shock-absorber-less buses, and into the countryside on buses with missing windows and with roofs piled high with striped plastic bags and boxes tied with string. I rarely flew on airplanes or took trains in China, but I considered myself lucky to have a bicycle when so many people I saw had access only to a mule and cart. I had filled and re-filled applications to make a long-distance telephone call at the city's main telecommunication office and waited long stretches of time in the lounge for a booth; and I had often passed grey-haired men, crouched beside pens and paper on city street corners, waiting to do trade with illiterate peasants or city dwellers who wished to send a letter to friends or family.

Still, I knew Hefei was well known as a centre of science and technology in China, partly because the University of Science and Technology of China had been moved at the height of the Cultural Revolution from Beijing to Hefei, then considered the countryside. "After thirty three years arduous trudge and furious climb," I read, the institution had won the right to be called "the cradle of China's science and technology and the attraction for young scientific and technical personnel with lofty ideas." The campus of the University of Science and Technology of China stretched beyond a large gate at the end of the road leading to our campus, Anyi Lu. The foreign teachers at our university occasionally visited the foreign teachers there. But we knew nothing about the research being done at the university. The neighbouring university figured into our conversations only when, frustrated by the lack of stimulation on campus, we congregated in Beth's room on a Friday night and speculated about what parties the well-fêted foreign teachers there were attending, or when we shared stories we had heard from our students about the student demonstrations for democracy that had taken place in 1986 on the campus of the university.

Nothing I had read so far set Hefei apart as a unique tourist spot not to be missed by a foreign traveller in China. Xi'an had its Terracotta Warriors and Suzhou its classical Chinese gardens. But what did Hefei have to merit its inclusion in a whirlwind tour of China? Perhaps there was some significant and intriguing event in the city's history?

My colleagues and students had often told me stories of ancient Hefei, tales of the upright official Bao Zheng, whose Memorial Temple with its "Spring of Probity"— named after a corrupt official who instantly got a headache when he drank from its waters—was a major tourist attraction in the city. And a famous battle fought on the site of the city's Xiaoyaojin Park in A.D. 208 between General Zhang Liao of the State of Wei and General Sun Quan of the State of Wu lived on in the communal memory in place-names such as Flying-Horse Bridge, over which Sun Quan took a flying leap as he retreated on his horse.

I had also learned from students and colleagues that Hefei had been a famous site during the Three Kingdoms period. Because of its location near the confluence of the Yangtze and Huai Rivers, the city had since ancient times served as an important trading centre for merchants travelling between the north and south of the country. Even the great Chinese historian, Sima Qian, had mentioned Hefei in his *Historical Records*.

I flipped to the section entitled "The Rise of the Ancient City – Hefei" and read:

> Bathed in the sunlight of the reform and opening of the
> the new age, today the ancient city of Hefei, which has

changed beyond recognition, is radiating the lustre of its
youth, becoming a bright pearl on the land of Jianghuai.

Apparently, Hefei had "suffered untold tribulations
and repeated wars" over the past two millenia. But with its
liberation on January 21, 1949, the city had been reborn as
"a beautiful modern industrial city in a spirit of changing
heaven and earth." Now the goal was to build Hefei into a
"comprehensive socialist modernized city."

I flipped back to a slogan I had come across in the
introductory paragraphs of the booklet. "Continuously
doing away with the old and creating the new"—the words
sounded more than a little incongruous when applied to
one of the earliest areas of the Yangtze Basin to be settled
by Sinitic peoples, peoples whose current linguistic and
cultural traits had been shaped more than seven hundred
years ago, during the southern Song dynasty.

I turned back to the table of contents. I was surprised
to find no mention of Hefei's arts, since Anhui Province
was the birthplace of the Huangmei Opera. I had learned
about the region's distinctive flower-drum folk opera from
an American scholar who had passed through the guest-
house on her way to do field research, and I had made my
own observations about the popularity of the art form.
Listening to the guest-house chef bellow, in his own
uniquely dissonant tones, arias from local operas as he
cooked the evening meal had become an inevitable part of
my daily routine. And on trips to the city centre, I had
often noticed merchants hawking tapes of Chinese operas
and grey-haired men crouching beside ghetto-blasters,
singing, in voices cracking with emotion, the songs to the
ancient tales. But the tourist booklet mentioned nothing
about these things, and the "charms and features" it did
highlight were described in tame and unevocative language laced through with political slogans.

I had almost finished the booklet; only two sections
remained. With fading hope that I would ever discover the

compelling charms and unique features of Hefei, I turned to the section entitled "Hefei city is forging ahead and bringing about changes day after day." I read with interest: "Taking the whole city as a big garden to build is the distinctive feature of the construction of Hefei." According to the description given in the booklet, paved paths led through woods and small greens, and newly built gardens and mini-parks adorned street corners, factories, schools, and residential quarters. "Rambling in these places," the writer mused, "you will feel as if you were in a fairyland."

I turned with anticipation to the final section, a description of the city's parks. The rhapsody, I quickly discerned, had begun.

> In the Round-the-City Park, the flowers, grass, and trees are verdant; and the bridges, waterside pavilions, and kiosks are facing each other. Moreover, hundred of birds often glide over the water and groups of sculptures on land form a delightful contrast. The newly-built Daoxiang, Xishan, Yinhe Parks, Juishi Fountain Square and places of historic interest and scenic beauty as Xiaoyaojin Park and Baohe Park add radiance and beauty to each other, which look like pearls mounted in the Round-the-City forest belt, thus making the Round-the-City Park be known as "a necklace with bright pearls." ... In the park, you will feel relaxed and happy and enjoy yourself so much as to forget to go home.

I wondered where the rhapsody would end. Flocks of aquatic birds twisted and glided over the water; mandarin, fish, and duck boats skimmed silently through river waters in the stillness of early morning, making you feel as if you were in a landscape painting; and at the end of the day, as the night fell, water and sky merged into one.

I remembered my first Sunday outing to the park. When Wu Li and I arrived, just after noon, the boaters were still out in full force. And not only boaters, but swimmers splashed jubilantly in the murky, polluted waters. Young lovers nestled together on blankets in the bushes near animal sculptures with names like "A Few Pandas Charmingly Naïve" and "An Awakening Lion," in search of that rare commodity in China—privacy. A photographer angled his camera left and right in an effort to capture the graceful lines of the Welcoming Sunlight Pavilion, set against a background of river and trees.

Wu Li and I had lingered in the park until sunset, strolling hand in hand, as good friends in China often do. As dusk descended, the whole scene before us faded into an ethereal splendour, "the water and the sky merging into one," as the writer of the tourist booklet had accurately described it. Just as we turned to leave, a white crane solemnly, majestically took its flight from out of the reeds where it had nested, hidden. "Taking the whole city as a big garden to build"—the slogan didn't match the one about building Hefei into "a comprehensive socialist modernized city." And yet, who was I to argue with the writer's efforts to re-imagine, in whatever language he chose, paradise? Hefei seemed the perfect place to take a rest from tourist sights, an ancient and a new garden in which the foreign traveller might commit a sin unthinkable to the Chinese by forgetting to go home.

Last Tango in Hefei

THE ENGLISH CORNER NIGHT SCHOOL was on Jingzhai Lu, right in the heart of the busiest section of Hefei. But since I travelled to the night school only during the twilight hours, I associated the place with the calm of that time of day. I would pass with my bicycle through the circular moon-gate into the courtyard within, where a group of middle-aged women would stand in a circle practising tai chi as the night fell. Not wanting to disturb their reverie, I would park and lock my bicycle as quietly as possible, then slip up the stairs to the staff room of the night school, where the director, Mr. Hua, and the other teachers would sit chatting and sipping tea out of communally owned cups grown stained from cold-water-only washings. At seven o'clock, the bell would ring and the teachers would all dash out of the room to meet their students.

The night-school students and my regular university students seemed to hail from different cultures, even worlds. While the university students dressed uniformly, following the campus trends of the day—the women

226

wearing tight, black, slightly flared pants and high-heeled black shoes, and the men, army green or navy blue Mao jackets, pants, and tousled hair—the night-school students wore no identifiable costume. They dressed according to the tastes of the city, the women in fashionable wool sweaters with brightly coloured voile scarves tied at their necks and flamboyant hairpieces, and the men, according to their own uniquely dashing chiaroscuro style, in black suit jackets, white shirts, tight black pants, and black shoes. The university students strode through campus confident in the knowledge that they were China's elite, the small fraction of China's primary-school students privileged to attend the country's universities. The night-school students, most of whom worked at factory jobs, walked the city streets with a certain self-possession gained from knowing that, to put it in Marxist terms, the means of production rested in their own hands.

The topics I covered at the university and at the night school reflected the fundamental difference in the temperaments of the two groups of students. At the university, I taught the kind of texts required in any introductory course in English literature, from Chaucer to T. S. Eliot, using various critical approaches to analyze them. At the night school, I spoke on subjects proposed by the students on the spur of the moment, usually practical subjects such as "How to Become Fluent in English" and general information topics like "Life in Canada," but also themes that appealed to their myth-hungry imagination—for example, the Genesis story of the Creation or the tale of Job's sufferings.

The night-school students found the story of the fall hilarious, especially the part where Adam blames Eve for his downfall. I never quite understood why. But they took Job's story very seriously, maybe because Job was the kind of character who could have appeared in a Chinese legend. A good old man fallen to ruin, for them he was the archetype of stoic suffering. His life spoke of the need for endurance that so permeated their own ethos.

227

When I told them Job's wife had urged him to curse God and die, they were shocked at this suggested act of rebellion, and their eyes grew wide with astonishment when, at the end of the story, God answered Job out of the whirlwind, saying, "Where wast thou when I laid the foundations of the earth?" The students quickly recognized the nature of Job's act of hubris as it was presented in the Bible story: it was the act of questioning somebody high above you, of challenging an incontestable authority. It was not something they approved of, but they were glad when Job was rewarded, too, since they felt it was only right that God recompense Job for whatever patience he had shown.

Similarly, the conversation at the city's English Corner, where the night-school students gathered to practise their English, reflected the gap between the simpler, more untamed imaginations of the adult students and the more educated imaginations of the younger university students. At the English Corner, you might be asked questions such as "Do you have a majesty?"—meaning "Do you have a Queen in Canada?"—or whether the winter was very cold in your country, or at what age girls were allowed to marry. You might even be asked if you believed in evil and hated "the snake," or if you thought it had "opened the world by its action." And when the questions were finished, you might be told you were "on the side of the angels" by a student who wanted to try out a newly acquired idiom.

But at the university English Garden, you would be asked which political system you thought was best for China, what your opinion was of China's economic reforms, and what you felt about the devaluation of knowledge. I remember especially the question of one intelligent young boy student who observed that the reigns of Queens Elizabeth and Victoria had witnessed a great flourishing of the arts, then asked if I thought societies led by women were more capable of producing great literature because women leaders were more able to maintain peace and social stability.

But at no time during the year did the rift between my two sets of students become more apparent than in the weeks just before my birthday. In China, there aren't any taboos about telling your age or the amount of your salary, as there are in North America. In China, your name is prefixed with *lao* (old) if you are older and *xiao* (little) if you are younger than the person you are with. As my Chinese teacher, Madame Liu, used to tell me proudly, she was once Xiao Liu but now she was Lao Liu. She didn't seem to have any regrets about growing older. Instead, she felt the satisfaction of finally "making it" and achieving some well-deserved status.

Still, there were some cases in which age was not mentioned. For example, how do you tactfully celebrate the birthday of a foreign teacher who has reached the age of thirty and is still not married? It was about the time of my birthday, I noticed, that Madame Liu asked me to join the 6:30 a.m. class she attended: disco for middle-aged ladies. I told her I would try to come the following day. Then it dawned on me: in China, a woman of thirty is considered middle-aged. Once when I introduced one of my students to a foreign teacher over forty with a toddler, the alarmed student whispered to me as soon as we were out of earshot, "Sarah's mother is old!"

I was middle-aged, maybe even what the same student would consider "old." I got the impression that my Chinese friends and colleagues felt my life was over. But the students still wanted to celebrate my birthday, the night-school students in their own way and the university students in their own way. I had heard from a fellow teacher that the night-school students planned to surprise me with an informal party in my room. The university students had planned a more elaborate event, a party called "Twelfth Night" after the play by Shakespeare and because my birthday was on the twelfth day of the month. Everyone invited to attend had to memorize a passage from Shakespeare, and, when the dance music stopped and the

flashlight beamed on them, they had to recite it. Twelfth
Night was a party for the elite: its organization was based
on the assumption that there was an intellectual class, and
that class could read Shakespeare as well as memorize long
passages from his plays.

The students debated where the dance party should be
held. If it took place in the large ballroom on the second
floor of the guest-house, they argued, strict security would
be needed in order to keep out crashers, or "bad elements." These "bad elements," mostly from the city's
night schools, had stormed the ballroom of the new Trade-
union Hall the previous term in the middle of Madame
Liu's favourite Strauss waltz. It wasn't worth the risk, they
decided, and so they chose the more modestly sized guest-
house dining room, big enough to hold about fifty people.
The students reserved the room and prepared the invitations with a passage from the play printed on them, changing a few key words, such as "love" to "life" and "kiss" to
"join," to suit their own purposes:

"What is life? 'Tis not hereafter;
Present mirth hath present laughter;
What's to come is still unsure:
In delay there lies no plenty;
Then come and join me, sweet and twenty,
Youth's a stuff will not endure."
(*Twelfth Night*, Act II, Scene iii)

You are invited to a "Twelfth Night" birthday party on
Friday May 12th at 7:30 at the Guest-House Dining
Room. Those in attendance must come as a character
from a Shakespeare play. No costumes are necessary,
unless desired, but you must bring with you some lines
spoken by your character. You may be asked to read or
recite these lines during the evening. Please bring any
tapes you like as the "Twelfth Night" celebration will
take the form of a dance party.

Please RSVP so that we will know how many people to
expect. . . .

I asked two of my students to make up an invitation list
by drawing names out of a hat, but they argued that
because Class Two was the most inhibited of the third-year
classes, its boys and girls would benefit most from receiving
the special invitation. It was an unexpectedly altruistic deci-
sion, and so I went along with it, leaving them to send out
the invitations.

Designed to have all the light and delightful touches of
a Shakespearean comedy, in the weeks before the party was
scheduled to take place Twelfth Night turned into a dark
nightmare of social relationships. The night-school students didn't really expect to be included, since many of
them could barely speak English let alone recite
Shakespeare. But the university students who didn't make
the guest list felt hurt. They could recite Shakespeare as
well as anyone, they reasoned, so why had they been
excluded?

As if to rub salt in the wound created by their exclu-
sion, the students of Class One appeared the morning of
the Twelfth Night celebration to decorate, sacrificially, the
guest-house dining room, hanging a labyrinth of bright
blue, yellow, and pink streamers from the ceiling in complex and beautifully elaborate patterns and raising the
room to a whole new level of beauty and design. When I
walked in, the students were singing and humming popular songs. A few were taking a break from decorating the
room to dance a waltz.

The night before the party, the night-school students
came to my room at six o'clock. One of them had made an
appointment with me to practise English, but when I
opened the door I was besieged with gifts and laughter and
cries of "Happy Birthday!" One student brought me a card
with a picture of a bride on the front. Another gave me
matching red silk pillowcases with the character for Double

Happiness woven on them. All the students had eaten their dinners, but they had made sure I had not. They cooked my birthday dinner themselves on a hotplate—noodles, the traditional Chinese symbol of longevity. When the long noodles were done, the students gathered around me for the pleasure of watching me struggle to eat them with my chopsticks.

After dinner, Miss Dai, a surprisingly Western-looking woman with curly black hair, a straight nose, and translucent white skin, consented to dance for us. It was a remarkable debut, and debut it was, for Miss Dai had said hardly a word the whole time I had known her, let alone so abandoned herself as to dance in front of an eager audience of twenty classmates. Miss Dai's dance wasn't an ordinary dance; it was a modern dance, Chinese style. The music, a gentle, harmonious, popular tune, drew her out of her seat like a call from another world. Her eyes, burning with the light of some inner fire, dazzled us as she rose to take the floor. Transformed by the music, Miss Dai became a swan, the most delicate and exquisite of creatures, moving gracefully, ethereally about the room. Then she was a leaf, blowing in the wind, as light as air. She bent backwards. She swung, then twirled, bending at the waist, legs stationary, torso circling round and round, eyes closed.

As the song came to an end, Miss Dai underwent her final metamorphosis, hurtling down from the empyrean of heaven to become fully human again, but now a girl so passionate and so sensuous that had my students not been so utterly absorbed in her performance, they might have been embarrassed. She opened her arms wide, thrust her chest forward, the smooth outline of her small breasts completely visible through her sweater, as she bent backward, her eyes fixed on a distant spot high above us all. She thrust out one hip and then another. She did a circling motion with her pelvis. She was sensuality itself, a living, vibrant sexual body.

When the dance was over, silence filled the room. Miss

Dai's sensuality, her energy, her passion—it took us all time to absorb the power of these unleashed in my small living quarters. Finally, Mr. Gao spoke: "That was the most beautiful dance I have ever seen!" Soon after Miss Dai's dance was over, the party came to an end. Her dance had transmuted the gay conviviality of the early evening into an atmosphere more sober and reflective. After some late-night songs, "Auld Lang Syne" and "Tonight Must Not Be Forgotten," we said goodbye. Outside, under the soft light of the spring moon, the students climbed onto their bicycles or began to walk towards home, in some distant part of the dark city.

Twelfth Night—I was almost dreading it now. So many complications had arisen in the planning of this innocent festival. Now the night had come and I stood at the door greeting my students, dressed in the new *qipao* Hu Xiaomei had the local dressmaker design for my birthday from a diamond-patterned gold and turquoise silk. At last, we were all assembled in the guest-house dining room, enclosed in our own little Illyria, a world of mistaken identities and unrequited passions in which the lunacy of love was just as compelling—and as perilous—as in Shakespeare's imagined kingdom. The girls stood on one side of the room, the boys on the other, as if to defy or perhaps deify love's power.

Mr. Gu set the tape machine going. The music filled the room and couples began to dance. They reminded me of Viennese waltzers at a funeral: they had mastered the steps perfectly but the spirit of gay abandon you might expect to find was supplanted by one of gravity, modesty, and a polite reserve. The music suddenly stopped and the flashlight beamed its light out into the crowd. Wu Li targeted Mr. Gu, our modern-day Hamlet. What a sombre beginning for the dance party, I thought. Couldn't Wu Li have flashed her light somewhere else? Then to everyone's surprise, Mr. Gu recited a passage from *Twelfth Night*:

If music be the food of love, play on,
Give me excess of it, that surfeiting,
The appetite may sicken, and so die.
That strain again. It had a dying fall;
O, it came o'er my ear like the sweet sound
That breathes upon a bank of violets,
Stealing and giving odor. Enough, no more.
'Tis not so sweet now as it was before. . . .

Shipwrecked on a shore of love, of Mr. Gu's passion surged then ebbed as the music resumed playing, this time a slightly mournful traditional Chinese melody. Apparently, each of my boy students felt obliged to dance with me on my birthday, and I was only at the beginning of the line-up. It would take the whole night to get through them all. Each more embarrassed than the last, my students moved me stiffly about the room as they made stilted conversation. At five feet nine inches, I towered above each of my partners as we danced then paused to listen to the latest soliloquy or sonnet. "Shall I compare thee to a summer's day?" recited Miss Qu as the flashlight illuminated her love-fevered face.

The party was winding down when Mr. Sun strode through the doors of the guest-house dining room, a vital energy bursting in on the staid scene with the power of new music. A tall, handsome, and unbelievably suave Chinese man, Mr. Sun was the heartthrob of the night school. His English wasn't bad, but he couldn't have recited Shakespeare if his life had depended on it.

The slow, soothingly melodic tunes of Chinese waltzes had been playing to prepare the dancers, psychologically, for the evening's end. But now a new beat shattered the calm: a tango. Only a few students knew the complex steps to this daring dance. Most drew back to take the seats lining the wall. Mr. Sun strode to my end of the room and offered me his hand. Soon only the two of us remained on the dance floor, Mr. Sun infusing life into my drooping, bedraggled body, so anesthetized by my previous dance partners.

Mr. Sun moved confidently up and down the whole length of the room in giant strides. I followed him, not out of skill, but commanded by the music and his own expert steps. He leaned low and threw me backwards into his arms, the top of my head parallel with the floor. The students clapped. Someone found a camera and began to take pictures. Primordial, outrageous—the beat of the tango drove us across the floor cheek to cheek, our joined arms pointing the way forward. I dipped low. Mr. Sun caught me. The pattern repeated itself as we strode back and forth.

It seemed the dance would never end, that Mr. Sun and I would continue forever to dip, bend, and stride across the guest-house dining room, making of Shakespeare's Illyria a mere fool's paradise of vapid, lovesick dreamers. Then, suddenly, the music stopped. My *qipao* was damp with the exertion of the dance. Mr. Sun stood coolly by me. I almost expected him, like a Chinese-style Rhett Butler, to pull at his white gloves and, having had his fill, walk in the opposite direction. Instead, he stood silently as Mr. Gu announced that there was time for one last recitation.

Wu Li stepped forth into the dim lights, their feeble glow casting shadows on the wall, just like tapers of old. I knew she had worked hard to memorize her passage. Now she seized her last chance to recite it before the party ended. She began:

> All the world's a stage,
> And all the men and women in it merely players;
> They have their exits and their entrances,
> And one man in his time plays many parts,
> His acts being seven ages. . . .

When Wu Li had finished her recitation, someone turned the lights off and everyone shuffled out of the room and went home to bed.

The Bee Pollen Cola Contest

TOWARDS THE END of my year in China, the Hefei Joint Bee Service, the Hefei English Learned Society, and *Anhui Youth Newspaper* launched the first Bee Pollen Nutrient Cola Cup English Knowledge Great Prize Match. Open to middle-school students, college students, "self-teaching youth," and other "English enthusiasts," the contest would be adjudicated, the advertisement claimed, by various English teachers from the city's universities, including "foreign experts and well-known people." The upper-level students had to submit a composition on any subject, or a translation, and the younger students an essay on "The Most Important Experience of My Life," to win prizes of five hundred *yuan*, two hundred *yuan*, fifty *yuan*, an English-Chinese dictionary, or a certificate of honour.

As one of only fifteen foreigners living in the city, I was used to being a hot commodity for advertising. Once when I left for a weekend trip to Beijing, colleagues from the English Corner Night School, where I taught a course in basic English once a week, offered to take me to the airport.

At their suggestion, we had our photo taken together in front of the main entrance. I noticed they were acting strangely, as if they might never see me again.

I knew Air China could be unreliable—if there had been any question in my mind about that, the emergency landing in Beijing on my arrival in China would have dispelled my doubts—but I did expect to live through the return flight. I had grown used to the Chinese custom, almost a ritual, of taking a photo as a way of formalizing an event. But I couldn't figure out what the occasion was. I was only going away for the weekend. Also, I didn't know these people well enough to get their names right when I said hello; why would they want to take such trouble to say goodbye to me?

A few weeks after I returned from Beijing, a student approached me on campus. "I saw your picture downtown," she said.

"Where?" I asked.

"In front of the English Corner Night School."

"Why was my picture there?"

"It was part of an advertisement for English classes at the night school," she said innocently.

To be a foreigner in Hefei was to be a celebrity. In a city of almost one million, you were known by virtually everybody. You were the "American student" or the "Canadian doctor" or the "Englishman who taught in Japan last year." You were invited to elaborate banquets by the province's minister of education at Christmas. One Chinese journalist with whom I had a casual conversation at the English Corner liberally quoted my opinions on China in an article published in the local newspaper. A radio journalist wanted to do a series of radio programs on my impressions of Chinese culture. Once, the foreign teachers at our university were invited to dance the first waltzes at the opening of a local disco. Another time, the two male foreign teachers at our university, both over fifty, were given free day passes to a new sports club, only to find the TV cameras already in place when they arrived, to film them lifting weights and pushing the pedals of the stationary bicycles.

It didn't really surprise me, then, that the night school was using the photograph—supposedly of me being received at the airport by members of the faculty—to advertise its English courses. By the time the Bee Pollen Cola Contest rolled around, I was used to being a personality around town. When the dean told me the four teachers at our university had been invited to attend the launching of the contest, I took it as just another celebrity engagement. A car would come for us at one o'clock.

Although it was April, on the day of the launching the weather turned so cold that I decided to wear my green People's Liberation Army coat. I had bought the coat at a local army-surplus store for thirty American dollars, and it was the warmest coat I had ever owned, though, as I discovered later, glaringly inappropriate for a slick, high-profile event that was being televised live province-wide. Dressed in the now-ratty old army coat with its cosy fake fur collar and its one-size-fits-none cut, I was certainly not in sync with a China based on commercial glitz, joint ventures, dapper foreign friends, and English. I must have seemed a quaint relic from a bygone age, a laughable reminder of some long-lost and highly unfashionable idealism. I dediced that, if the TV cameras zeroed in on me as the final toast was being raised, I would try to hide behind my bottle of Bee Pollen Cola.

Scholars from all over the city had gathered together under the umbrella of the Hefei English Learned Society for the contest launching. After our dean had proudly flaunted his four foreign teachers in front of various highly placed Party members, including the vice-governor of the province, he left us to circulate until the speeches began. As I wandered around the drafty, high-ceilinged room, obviously designed for old-style communist meetings of hundreds of comrades, I met a doctor of Chinese medicine who, like everyone else, was studying English. Dr. Tao could tell I was suffering from the last vestiges of a bronchial infection and offered to come to my rooms to treat me.

"But no, it's too much trouble," I protested. "What can I offer in return?"

"Practise English?" he asked. I nodded my head in agreement.

A mathematics teacher from a local high school, a professor of physics from the city's top science university, a tai chi master—all said they were members of the Hefei English Learned Society and honoured to attend the launching of the Bee Pollen Cola Contest. The Hefei English Learned Society seemed to be an association with branches sheltering everyone in Hefei society who loved learning English. Experts in every field of knowledge, ancient and modern, had been brought into a close circle of relationships by Bee Pollen Cola and its main promoters, the Joint Bee Society.

The Joint Bee Society—the name conjured in my mind images of masses of busy bee-like workers marching in broad phalanx-like formations across Tiananmen Square on May Day. Or it brought to mind a relic of the Qin dynasty pictured on a postcard I had received from a friend long before I ever thought of teaching in China, featuring the Army of Terracotta Warriors unearthed at Xi'an, representing nameless vassals of a once-powerful emperor. The name suggested masses of busy people, a whole society of workaholics impelled by some primordial impulse to run themselves into the ground performing monumentally difficult tasks *en masse*, each one serving as a crucial link in a long and highly intricate chain of endeavour.

An announcement rang out over the PA system. It was time for the bees to alight, each one in its place, with a bottle of Bee Pollen Cola in front of it. Reserved, in typical Chinese fashion, for the important guests, the head table was covered with a white tablecloth and laid with bowls of fruit and candy. The TV cameras targeted it, and the lights shone brightly on it.

The rest of the bees sat at the tables lining both sides of the room, perpendicular to the head table. These were also spread with white tablecloths but decorated with smaller and fewer bowls of fruit, candies, and nuts. The very slight difference between the tables laid out for the greater and the lesser bees seemed to reflect an unstated ethic—that everyone should be treated equally though not exactly the same.

The Queen Bee, a veteran of the Long March with battle scars from the Japanese invasion, took her seat. Other Party officials sat near her at the main table. One of the Joint Bees ushered me to the same table and seated me on the right of the Queen Bee. In her personal relations just another friendly grandmother, the Queen, who had retired from politics years ago, cut a formidable figure when she addressed the gathering. Like many cadres of her generation, she shouted out her sentences in a military fashion, using a rhetorical style intended to mobilize the masses.

"Greetings, comrades!" she began in Chinese. "We are here today, in this new period of opening up and reforms, to promote knowledge through the study of English. China's economic growth depends on it. Begun in 1979 and given momentum by last year's Thirteenth Party Congress, the economic reform of the open door period is progressing satisfactorily," she volleyed forth. She cited a profusion of statistics to prove her point, then went on to say: "In this province we have been honoured to be the first to implement the new agricultural reforms, which have proven successful all over China—the household responsibility system. Today, we are honoured to carry forward the opening up of China for development and knowledge through the study of English, by launching the Bee Pollen Nutrient Cola Cup English Knowledge Great Prize Match. Today we salute you, comrades, teachers, and students, for your efforts to be at the vanguard of the new developments and reforms. And so I toast you now!"

Then Comrade Queen Bee poured some Bee Pollen Cola into her glass and raised it to the cameras. "Gua gua jiao!" (Extremely good!), she barked. "Gan bei!" (Bottoms up!).

All around the room, the learneds raised their glasses and dutifully downed the syrupy brown liquid. "Gan bei!" they responded as one voice. Another hour of speeches and Bee Pollen Cola was officially launched.

Several weeks after the official launching of the contest, the results came in. At the Foreign Guest-house, we had received silk-bound invitations asking us to be members of "the English Test Results Commenting Board," but everyone except Dan was too busy to have time for the bees. I might have been interested—I was curious to know what China's youth were thinking—but I had been struck down by another attack of bronchitis.

As I lay in bed in a daze, succumbing to the illness despite the powerful antibiotics I had finally managed to get from a chest specialist at a local hospital, my students slipped into my bedroom and left small gifts of chocolates, nuts, and candy, including my favourite, homemade peanut brittle, on my bedside table. Then, one evening, as I woke up from my fevered sleep, I saw a middle-aged man sitting in the chair by my bed. He looked vaguely familiar, but I couldn't place him.

Was I hallucinating? Was the man an angel come to release me forever from this grimy, gritty world of airborne coal dust? His radiant complexion and trim, healthy form did seem to be gifts of another world more perfect than this. Wouldn't such a middle-aged man in a trim blue Mao suit be the most suitable possible emissary from the other world to dying souls in China? Once when I had offered my condolences to a Chinese friend who had lost his wife, he had answered, without a trace of emotion, "Do not be sorry. Death is a part of life." Could it be in the same spirit of detached unconcern that this man had come to usher me away?

"Dr. Tao?" I asked, suddenly placing him. "From the Hefei English Learned Society?" I stuttered, punctuating every two words with the staccato bass of my chesty cough.

"Yes, it is the same," he replied. "I heard you were sick. I have come to bring treatment." He reached into a big brown bag and brought out several small and medium-sized packages wrapped in brown paper and tied with string. He lined them up on my desk. "Traditional Chinese medicine," he said. "Mostly herbs."

"How can I thank you?" I asked.

"Just drink," he said, as he mixed up the first brew of herbs. "Three times a day," he added, then began to write instructions on each package in simple Chinese characters for "one," "two," "three," or however many times a day I needed to take the herb. "Now for qigong," he announced. "No, your qi is not good. If so, you would have no sickness. You need better energy from the earth. Now follow me, and fill up your mind with nothing."

I sat up in the bed and watched him. Palms down, he moved his hands in a kind of rubbing motion through the air. "That's the qi, " he explained. Then he bent down to the ground and made a scooping motion, as if he were drawing energy up from the earth. Finally, he spread the energy over his body in a kind of sweeping motion.

I stood up and followed him through as much of the exercises as I could. I was amazed that I could feel heat in my hands when I did the rubbing motion.

When I had finished, I crawled back into my bed and pulled my shiny pink satin quilt over me.

"Tomorrow, you will feel better," he assured me. "Now I must go."

To my surprise, the next day I did feel better. In two more days, I was out of bed. It was hard to know whether the antibiotics or Dr. Tao's visit brought about my miracle recovery. Within a week, I was back teaching classes. On my first day back, the dean approached me in the hall of the Foreign Languages Department.

"Saturday at one p.m. the car will come for you," he said. "Attendance, of course, is optional, but I thought you might want to know there is a meeting of the Hefei English Learned Society to award prizes to the winners of the Bee Pollen Cola Contest. I suppose," he laughed, "it's another kind of propaganda!"

"Saturday at one p.m? I'll be ready. I've been looking forward to it."

The ceremony was unremarkable. The Queen Bee wasn't there; some lower-level official had been sent to preside over the meeting instead. After all the suspense built up by the launching, it was rather anticlimactic to hear the titles of the winning papers in the "Most Important Experience of My Life" category: "My Trip to Our Capital City, Beijing," "My Hometown: Growing Up in the Countryside," and "The Day I Decided to Become a Scientist." Dan and I were relieved when the meeting ended and the car dropped us back at the guest-house.

It didn't seem remarkable at the time, but now and then I think about the Bee Pollen Cola Contest. Once in a while I even take out the advertisement, with its official red star of China stamped on the back, look at it, and wonder what I would have written had I been a middle-school student in China during the spring of 1989, or what I would write now, looking back, on the most important experience of my life in China.

Sometimes, late at night, when I am drifting off to sleep, I compose in my mind an essay in prose so simple yet so suggestive that it reminds me of a Chinese brushstroke painting, rendering a tranquil world of imagination where peace, harmony, and balance reign. Sometimes the foreground of this painting is dominated by a single cherry blossom. Sometimes there are bees on the blossom and sometimes there are not. But students always appear in the painting, night-school students and university students. At first, you cannot see them: in the composition of a brushstroke painting, absences speak as loudly as presences,

Sandra Hutchison

white spaces are as powerful as colour. But if you look closely at the empty spaces on the page, pure as the snow on top of a holy mountain or a dewdrop on a slowly opening, delicate red rose, you will see inscribed not only their faces but their dreams.

Epilogue
A Chest Full of Ming

THE CHEST MUST HAVE SAT in the garage a full year before I could bring myself even to look at it. Then, gradually, I began to think about unpacking it, sifting the wheat from the chaff, separating the cheap tourist souvenirs I had picked up—the bean sculpture; the chicken basket; the handkerchiefs inscribed with the names Beijing, Nanjing, Hangzhou; the plastic cat with a thermometer in its belly—from the exquisite porcelain vases given to me by the university in thanks for my services and the collection of meticulously painted china courtiers and concubines I had bought in Shanghai, all imitation Ming. I hoped the foot-high Tang dynasty-style horse my night-school students had given me and the shell sculpture my third-year students had presented to me on Teachers' Day were still in one piece.

Somehow I knew they would be. Cloud had packed the chest, not once but several times, arranging and rearranging the contents for maximum use of space, wrapping and rewrapping to add extra padding for the fragile items.

"General Cloud" I called her, since she supervised with military efficiency not only the packing of my chest, but every detail of my hasty departure from China in June 1989, after most of my students had fled for the safety of home and most of my colleagues didn't want to associate with a foreigner, let alone worry about a chest immoderately stuffed, mostly with items of little material value.

I met Cloud after a lecture on Canadian literature I gave to the English Garden students. Cloud had studied in Shandong with one of the handful of university teachers who, having pursued graduate studies in the field in Canada, now specialized in Canadian Studies. Professor Song had infused into Cloud a love of everything Canadian, and after my lecture she clung to me, asking questions. Later, when she visited my room, Cloud showed me a photo of herself with Professor Song standing beneath a Canadian flag tacked to the wall, a kind of souvenir of battle in a foreign land.

Cloud's knowledge of Canada was broad, encompassing a wide range of obscure facts. For example, she knew a surprising amount about the Fathers of Confederation, and she had somehow divined the most abstruse details of constitutional reform. Since the university library had almost no books on Canada, I sometimes wondered how Cloud had come to possess such learning. Information about the West seeped into China, it seemed, in the same way the parched earth soaks up every available drop of water after a rain. Cloud's plan was to pursue graduate studies in Canadian History; her dream was to write a history of Canada that wove together past and present in a patchwork fashion, such as you might find in a Quebec-style braided rug woven from brightly coloured pieces of leftover wool.

The first few times Cloud visited my room, we talked about Canadian history non-stop for two or three hours. Before long, she was coming by regularly just to chat. By the time the class strike was called at our university, Cloud had gotten into the habit of dropping in daily to listen to the VOA news broadcast on my shortwave radio. The magnolia trees in the Chinese garden had passed their full bloom. The weather grew hot and humid, the air close as a lover's kiss. Cloud and I often sat on the balcony of my room discussing the future of China and listening to the rain make music as it fell on the broad leaves of the *ba-jiao* trees outside my window.

On May 20, the day martial law was declared, Cloud insisted that I pack my bags. "How could I get all this into a suitcase?" I asked, waving my hand at the cluttered room in a gesture of hopelessness.

"I know someone who can help," Cloud said. "He can make a chest big enough for all these things."

Mr. Wu's shop was around the corner from the campus health clinic, not far from the east gate. That afternoon, Cloud and I visited his shop to ask how much it would cost to buy a made-to-order wooden chest large enough to hold all my possessions. The price was reasonable, so we ordered the chest. But when we asked when it would be ready, Mr. Wu refused to answer. As the only carpenter on campus, he didn't seem to feel obliged to set firm deadlines for the delivery of his products.

In the next few days, whenever I rode through the east gate of the campus I glanced in the direction of Mr. Wu's shop. One warm afternoon, I saw him sleeping in the shade on his workbench. And once, late at night, I heard a furious racket of hammering and sawing coming from the shop, as if Mr. Wu had taken it upon himself to build up the New China and was working against the clock to finish the job.

While we waited for Mr. Wu to finish the chest, Cloud and I sorted through my belongings, beginning with the books and papers. I could not bring myself to throw out the sampling of student essays I had saved, plagiarism and all, or the silk-tassled invitation to the Bee Pollen Cola Contest. Nor could I part with the print of Confucius I had bought in his birthplace, Qufu, or the many notes written by students and friends on scraps of paper and left with Lao Zheng, notes such as,

> Dear Dr.,
> We return your book with the same spirit of grace and bounteousness in which it was given. We wish you happy, lucky forever. We will see you in class tomorrow!

or,

> Ha Qisen:
> Women's Day celebration is tomorrow. If you want to come, please tell us and we will arrange for a car. Don't stand on ceremony. Remember: "Ladies hold up half the sky!"

And then there were my books, the books I had brought from Canada and the others I had acquired in China. I put aside for packing the small comic books Wu Hong loved to read; she had given her whole collection to me, thinking they would help me with my Chinese. Then I pulled from my bookshelf the hefty three-volume set of *A Dream of Red Mansions* given to me by some of the students at Fuyang Teachers' College, though I could never hope to read it through.

When Cloud and I finished with the books and papers, we started on my clothes: the gold and turquoise *qipao* Hu Xiaomei had a local seamstress make for my birthday; the fashionable sweaters and the white silk pyjamas Daoling had bought me in Shanghai; the gold scarf Wu Jiao had given me in his bid to win my hand in helping him go abroad; and the curious "split pants," a Chinese substitute for diapers, I had bought at a local roadside market. Finally, I placed my beloved People's Liberation Army coat in the chest. No matter how worn and tattered it was, I could never give it up.

Last, we got to the handicrafts and the china, a mountain of mostly useless and un-aesthetic objects: the painted clay opera figurines Ding Liang had given me, a host of sandalwood fans various visitors to my rooms had presented to me, a small wooden carving of a juggler balancing a horizontal pole, a set of hand-painted ducks, a brown china monkey, a black horse, and a laughing Buddha, to name only a few.

I added to the take-home pile my well-used dragon mug, a package of holy-mountain tea, and a box of health-inducing royal jelly I had bought in Hefei's largest department store. Next, I selected several tapes of Chinese waltzes and rock music and an imitation-gold medallion commemorating the year of the snake. Then I wrapped in some tissue paper the cloisonné week rings Sun Li and I had bought in the Friendship Store in Shanghai and the Mao button the Zhang family had given me when I had visited the Evergreen Commune.

Mr. Wu delivered the chest just after lunch several days after we had ordered it. That afternoon, Cloud and I packed the items we had set aside and closed the chest. Despite its large dimensions, not everything fit in the chest, so we packed the remaining valuables in a couple of striped plastic bags, for storage at San Chang until I returned to China. Then we pushed the heavy chest in front of my tea table. For the time being, we decided, it would make a good chair.

Cloud and I sat side by side on top of the chest drinking tea. My shortwave radio blared out the latest report on the hunger strike in Tiananmen Square, but I could tell that Cloud wasn't really listening. I wondered if she was dreaming about Canada. Perhaps she viewed the chest as the ark of my salvation in which I would sail, at the appointed hour, back to my own country, her promised land. I knew how much she wanted to come with me, though she never spoke of it.

Two weeks after we had packed the chest, I was gone.

Cloud and I kept in touch for a while, then stopped writing for a whole year. Not long after I had unpacked the chest, Cloud wrote to tell me she would be coming to Toronto for a conference on Canadian Studies. But by the time she arrived several months later, I had moved away again. I never did have the chance to ask Cloud how Canada compared with the country of her imagination.

Friends told me that soon after her visit to Toronto, Cloud had married Professor Song's son, who had won a scholarship to study in Canada, and that she had been accepted for graduate studies in Women's History at Boston University. Now, they told me, Cloud was trying desperately to cross the border to Canada, but she couldn't get a visa and feared she would be separated from her husband for years.

After that I lost track of Cloud. I don't know where she lives now, or if she succeeded in getting across the border to join her husband. I don't know where she is, but I wish I could find her. It is time for me to pack again, and I could use her help. I've given away many of the things I was once so reluctant to part with. As time passed, I began to see them in their true light: as cheaply made tourist souvenirs. But they made perfect gifts for friends who had never been to China and hoped to travel there someday. I've abandoned the chest Mr. Wu built for me. It didn't survive the journey well. A few boards came loose, and it looks as if it would burst if it were packed as full as it once was. Now I'm going back to China, this time to Hong Kong, to live in a house by the sea. I am told it looks north to the shores of the mainland and that sampans smuggling goods made in China sail in the waters nearby. This time I'm planning to pack only a small chest of valuables. I bought a beautiful rosewood box the other day in Chinatown—a collector's item, I am told. It is the size of a small jewel box and looks like an imitation chest, with gold handles on its sides and an ornate gold lock on the front with a key so small you have to be careful it doesn't disappear in your pocket. On the top of the box gleams, also in gold, the Chinese character for longevity. Very auspicious. I think I'll call it my longevity box.

It is big enough to hold everything essential to my future: the bright red paper-cutting of the characters for Double Happiness that Madame Liu sent me when I married last spring, a small vial of earth from my grandmother's garden, a crystal paperweight with a loon carved into it given to me by my father, some dried yellow petals from my mother's backyard rosebushes, and my tiny cloisonné swan, just big enough to carry in its belly all the tears I hope I will ever cry.

I've given up transporting large chests filled with belongings to and from China. Memories are a heavy enough load. I travel eastward, westward—really it doesn't matter. All paths lead somehow to the same room, a small room but large enough for at least two, down a winding stone path, just past a circular moon-gate veiled by a delicate cluster of plum branches, at the heart of an ancient Chinese garden. Wherever I am, the garden calls to me. Its jasmine flowers bloom so fragrantly, and its magnolia trees shine, luminous, in the mid-afternoon sun. A pond crowded with water lilies lies so still, just waiting for a crane to alight. And around each twist of the garden's paths, an unexpected view beckons, startlingly new and breathtaking.

Sometimes, as I walk through the garden, I hear the plucking of a *pipa* or the melancholy wail of the *erhu* in the distance. But mostly I hear wind and rain, wind carrying the scent of jasmine and rain sounding the chimes of memory, delicately, persistently, until I can be almost anywhere anytime I choose, until I forget that the earth is more than one country. East, West—both leading me home.

251

About the Artist

Joseph Lo has practised Chinese calligraphy for more than eighteen years. In order to understand this delicate art better, he also learned Chinese seal engraving, poetry, painting and traditional music. His work has been seen in Hong Kong in joint exhibition with his teacher, Chan Man Kit. He was among the artists represented in the E-merging Cultures exhibition at Winnipeg's Main/Access Gallery in November, 1993.

A member of the Hong Kong Calligrapher's Association, Lo received third prize in the international Chinese calligraphy contest organized by the Radio Broadcasting Voice of Free China in 1985.

Lo was the Artist-in-residence of the Winnipeg Art Gallery in 1994. He was the instructor of Chinese Calligraphy in WAG, and the Art of Chinese Brush in Winnipeg School Division No. 2. He is also a freelance graphic designer and a well-known poet in the local Winnipeg Chinese community. He serves as volunteer Principal of the non-profit Chinese school of the Institute of Chinese Language, Culture and Arts, and is one of the directors of the Winnipeg Chinese Culture and Community Centre.

About the back cover:
The title of this piece is called *Act rather than Say*. The trail left by the snail is a grass style Chinese character which means "a lot" or "abundant." This is a piece of work simply combining Chinese Calligraphy and brush work. Snail is a soundless organism. It moves slowly. No matter how fast or slow one's pace, the point is to Act it out rather than Say.